Gnosis and Faith in Early Christianity

Gnosis and Faith in Early Christianity

An introduction to gnosticism

Riemer Roukema

SCM PRESS

Translated by John Bowden from the Dutch *Gnosis en geloof in het vroege christendom. Een inleiding tot de gnostiek*, published 1998 by Uitgeverij Meinema, Zoetermeer, The Netherlands.

0 334 02773 X

This edition first published 1999
by SCM Press
9–17 St Albans Place, London N1 0NX

SCM Press is a division of
SCM-Canterbury Press Ltd

Typeset by Regent Typesetting, London
and printed in Great Britain by
Biddles Ltd, Guildford and King's Lynn

Contents

Preface   xi

Part I A first orientation   1

1. Introduction   3
    1. Gnosis as awareness and redemption   3
    2. Sources of gnosticism   4
        2.1 The books of Nag Hammadi   4
        2.2 The Gnostic Berlin Codex and other
            Coptic texts   6
        2.3 The church fathers   7
    3. The structure of this book   10

2. Irenaeus on the origin of the heresies   13
    1. Simon the magician   14
        1.1 Traditions about Simon the magician   14
        1.2 Analysis and interpretation of the myth of
            Simon and Helen   17
    2. Menander of Antioch   23
    3. Irenaeus, gnostics and gnosis   24

3. A sermon from the Nag Hammadi books   26
    1. The Exegesis on the Soul   26
    2. The Exegesis on the Soul compared with
       'Simon and Helen'   28

3. The Exegesis on the Soul, gnosis and
   Christianity   30

4. Refinements of the gnostic myth   32

   1. Satornilus of Antioch   32
      1.1 The myth of Satornilus   32
      1.2 Notes on the myth of Satornilus   34
   2. The Secret Book of John   36
      2.1 The tradition of the Secret Book of John   36
      2.2 The content of the Secret Book of John   38
      2.3 Retrospect on the Secret Book of John   48
   3. Passwords for the return of the soul   49
      3.1 The journey along the planets   49
      3.2 The First Revelation of James   50
      3.3 Mark the Gnostic   51
      3.4 The Ophites   51

Part II Backgrounds to gnosticism   55

5. The origin and purpose of life   57

   1. Lucius Annaeus Seneca   57
   2. Clement of Rome   59
   3. Akabya ben Mahalalel   59
   4. Philo of Alexandria   60
   5. Theodotus, pupil of Valentinus   60
   6. Tertullian's verdict   62

6. The Jewish religion   64

   1. The first chapters of Genesis   65
      1.1 The creation of the world and the first
          human beings   65
      1.2 Notes on the first chapters of Genesis   66
   2. The curse on the earth and human destiny   68

3. God and the heavenly powers   70
    3.1 The one God, the angels and the devil   70
    3.2 God, Wisdom and the Word   71
    3.3 God as man and the son of man   72
    3.4 God's unity and the powers alongside God   73
4. 'Knowledge' in Judaism   73

7. **Plato, Philo and Platonic philosophy**   75

1. Plato's dialogues   76
    1.1 The doctrine of ideas and the purpose of life   76
    1.2 To attain knowledge is to remember knowledge   76
    1.3 The origin of the world according to the *Timaeus*   77
    1.4 The supreme divine principle   79
    1.5 Notes on Plato's dialogues   80
2. Philo's exposition of the books of Moses   81
    2.1 Philo of Alexandria and Greek philosophy   81
    2.2 *The Creation of the World*   82
    2.3 Notes on *The Creation of the World*   84
    2.4 Plurality in the one God   85
    2.5 The origin and destiny of souls   87
    2.6 Retrospect on Philo of Alexandria   87
3. Two Middle Platonic philosophers   88
    3.1 Alcinous's introduction to the teaching of Plato   88
    3.2 Numenius of Apamea   89
4. Retrospect on Plato and Middle Platonism   91

8. **The mystery religions and early Christianity**   93

1. The worship of Isis and Osiris   94
    1.1 Plutarch of Chaeronea on Isis and Osiris   94
    1.2 Apuleius of Madaura on the worship of Isis and Osiris   95

2. Early Christianity   97
    2.1 Jesus of Nazareth, Son of God   97
    2.2 The dissemination of faith in Jesus Christ   99
    2.3 Faith in Jesus Christ as the true knowledge   100

Part III A closer look at Gnosticism   103

9. A form of Hellenized Christianity   105

    1. The highest God, the Creator and the world   105
    2. The creation of human beings   109
    3. The Redeemer and the redemption of human
        beings   111
    4. Gnostics, the Old Testament and creation   114
    5. The Platonizing of Hellenistic religions   118
    6. What is gnosis, what is a gnostic, and what
        is gnosticism?   120
    7. Gnosis as a form of the Hellenization of
        Christianity   124

10. Some gnostic and related teachers   126

    1. Cerinthus   126
    2. Basilides, Isidorus and the Basilidians   127
    3. Valentinus   129
    4. Ptolemaeus   130
    5. Heracleon   132
    6. Theodotus   133
    7. Justin the Gnostic   134
    8. Marcion   136
    9. Mani   138

11. Some gnostic and related texts   140

    1. The Gospel of Thomas   140
    2. The Gospel of Philip   142

3. The Gospel of Truth   143
4. The Treatise on the Resurrection   145
5. The Hymn of the Pearl   145

Part IV Christian faith and gnosis   149

12. The gnosis of some church fathers   151

  1. Clement of Alexandria   151
  2. Origen   153
  3. Evagrius of Pontus   156
  4. The early church and its gnostic tradition   157

13. Gnosis assessed   158

  1. Is not God the Father at the same time the
     Creator?   159
  2. Did Jesus Christ have a gnostic message?   163
  3. Was gnosticism elitist?   168

Bibliography   171

Notes   178

Index of texts   203
  1. Bible   00
  2. Jewish writings   00
  3. Christian (including gnostic) writings   00
  4. Greek and Roman authors   00
Index of names and subjects   00

Preface

The ongoing discussions about the place of gnosis in early and present-day Christianity, together with a request by the publisher, led me to write this book. Earlier versions of the first nine chapters, or of individual chapters, have been read by Esther de Boer, C. A. Bos, C. Houtman, Gijs Jonkers and Marijke van Riessen. I am grateful to them for their critical comments; these have led to a large number of changes and additions.

I have made some small additions and corrections to the Dutch text for this English edition. I hope that this book will clarify the relationship between Christianity and gnosis, both in antiquity and at the present time.

Kampen, 1 September 1999
Riemer Roukema

Part I   A first orientation

I

Introduction

1. Gnosis as awareness and redemption

This book is about 'gnosis' or, to use another term, 'gnosticism'. What can and what cannot be classified under 'gnosis' or 'gnosticism' and whether these terms are suitable designations for the tendency that they denote is a matter for discussion. However, to begin with I shall describe them provisionally as if there were no such discussion.

Gnosticism is usually understood as a very varied religious movement from the first centuries of our era. In this tendency people were concerned to discover the purpose of life in a particular form of gnosis. Gnosis is a Greek word which can be translated 'knowledge' or 'insight'. Those who were receptive to this gnosis got insight into the being of the most high God and into the origin of various other spiritual powers. This gnosis related to the origin of the world, the purpose of life on earth, and the way in which a human being can achieve spiritual redemption. According to this gnosis human beings have a slumbering heavenly nucleus in them which comes from the most high God. However, they have forgotten this original heavenly origin of part of their inner being. During life on earth it is important to become conscious of it again and thus, through the true gnosis, to restore contact with the divine. In this way, human beings who are open to gnosis can find the way back on high again.

The terms 'gnosis' and 'gnosticism' are not everyday ones, but what they denote is enjoying a degree of popularity. 'Gnostic' books from antiquity have been published in translation and books about gnosticism are appearing. The discovery of a collection of ancient writings called 'gnostic' in Nag Hammadi in Egypt in 1945 gave powerful impetus to an interest in gnosticism. Apart from this revealing discovery, all kinds of other gnostic witnesses have been preserved, which are again attracting attention. There are people who can identify with gnostic views and feel more akin to them than to the 'catholic' and 'orthodox' Christianity which also arose in this time.

This book contains an introduction to gnosticism, according to the meaning that is usually attached to it. It is about different gnostic teachers and groups, about their myths and other kinds of texts, and about the religious and philosophical background to their gnosis. The question is also raised whether the designations gnosis and gnosticism are so suitable for this subject.

2. *Sources of gnosticism*

We are dependent on all kinds of ancient texts for our knowledge of gnosticism. To provide a first orientation, here is an introduction to a number of these ancient works and where possible to their authors. I shall use the designation 'gnostic' here in its current meaning, but regularly put it in quotation marks. However, because the constant use of quotation marks with these words can in the long run prove disturbing, I shall also often omit them.

2.1. *The books of Nag Hammadi*

The writings which were found in 1945 in a jar in Nag Hammadi in Egypt are of great importance. This 'library' comprises twelve books bound in leather (in Latin called *codices*, the plural of *codex*), plus eight pages of a thirteenth book. The pages of these books are papyrus and contain fifty-two Coptic texts, some of which appear more than once. So this collection numbers forty-five writings, ten of which are severely damaged, while the rest are reasonably legible.

Most texts have a 'gnostic' content. Some texts were already known, but the vast majority were not.

Many of the individual writings are attributed to persons who are known from the New Testament. They bear titles like the Gospel of Thomas, the Gospel of Philip, the Secret Book of John, the Prayer of the Apostle Paul, the Revelation of Paul, the Revelation of Peter, the Secret Book of James, the Revelation of James (there are two of these) and the Teachings of Silvanus. Other works bear the names of Old Testament figures: the Revelation of Adam, the Paraphrase of Shem, the Second Treatise of the Great Seth, the Three Steles of Seth, Melchizedek. Titles with non-biblical names are Zostrianus, Marsanes, the Sentences of Sextus. Yet other titles are the Gospel of Truth, the Exegesis on the Soul, the Gospel of the Egyptians, the Dialogue of the Saviour, the Testimony of Truth, The Interpretation of Knowledge.

We do not know who wrote these works. The fact that a large number of them have been attributed to known figures does not in itself mean that these works were really written by them. In antiquity people thought it quite permissible to write a book under someone else's name.

The original language of these works, which have been handed down in Coptic, is Greek. With some exceptions, however, the Greek texts have been lost. The original Greek versions generally come from the second and third centuries. The Coptic manuscripts which have been preserved date from the fourth century.

References to individual writings look like this: Revelation of Peter (NHC VII, 3), 79, 22–31. NHC stands for Nag Hammadi Codex. The Roman number VII is the number of the codex. The figure which follows (3) indicates the place that this writing occupies in the codex. Then come the page of the codex (79) and the lines on the page (22–31).

2.2. *The Gnostic Berlin Codex and other Coptic texts*

Apart from the texts from Nag Hammadi, other Coptic texts have been found which bear witness to a form of gnosticism. In 1896 the Egyptological Department of the Berlin Museum acquired a papyrus codex in Cairo which contains four writings that have not been completely preserved. Their titles are: the Gospel of Mary (Mary Magdalene is meant here); the Secret Book of John; the Wisdom of Jesus Christ; the Act of Peter. Apart from the last very short text the whole manuscript was published only in 1955. Other versions of the Secret Book of John and the Wisdom of Jesus Christ have been found in Nag Hammadi. Some lines of the Gospel of Mary are also known in Greek. The writings on this papyrus probably come from the second century. As with the Nag Hammadi texts, the authors of these writings too are unknown, and the works have been translated from Greek into Coptic. The papyrus probably comes from the region of Achmim in ancient Egypt and was written in the fourth or fifth century.

Because the papyrus was kept in Berlin, it has been called the Berlin papyrus (Berolinensis Gnosticus). Because it has been given the number 8502 in that museum, it is referred to as BG 8502. This abbreviation is sometimes given after the title of one of its writings.

Two extensive Coptic books on parchment with a gnostic content were found as early as the eighteenth century. They are named the Askew Codex (Codex Askewianus) and the Bruce Codex (Codex Brucianus) after their purchasers. The first codex contains a long work with the title Pistis Sophia, i.e. Faith-Wisdom. This describes how after his resurrection from the dead Jesus has long conversations with his disciples, among whom Mary Magdalene occupies a prominent position. The second codex contains the Book of the Great Mystery, also called the two Books of Jeu, in which the risen

Jesus initiates his apostles into the knowledge of the truth. This is followed by two fragments of prayers, a third fragment and a description of the heavenly spheres and their inhabitants, among whom Seth occupies an important place. These works, too, were originally written in Greek. They come from the third century; the manuscripts are dated in the fourth or fifth centuries.

2.3. *The church fathers*

In the second century there were believers in the Christian communities who felt attracted to the gnostic 'knowledge'. In fact, to begin with there was not always a clear dividing line between 'catholic' and 'gnostic' Christians. However, in the course of the second century, with the spread of gnosticism, the contours of the 'catholic' church began to be drawn more sharply.[1] From the middle of this century the church produced a number of bishops and scholars who attacked these gnostics in writings. As part of their discussions of the deviant views they summarized many of their texts or quoted parts of them. So it is part of the irony of history that unintentionally these 'church fathers' have become important witnesses to the heresies that they wanted to dispute. Moreover it is remarkable that some of these authors, too, came into conflict with the church to which they belonged.

Irenaeus must be mentioned first.[2] He came from Asia Minor, probably from Smyrna, but lived in Lugdunum in Gaul, a Roman city which is now called Lyons. There was a Christian community here, and Irenaeus became its bishop in 177 or 178. He wrote a work in five volumes to refute the gnostic heresies: its title was *Disputation and Refutation of the Wrongly So-called Gnosis*, or also *Against the Heresies*. The first book begins with a lengthy account of the views of 'the gnostic Ptolemaeus, a disciple of Valentinus. After that follow the teachings which were attributed to, for example, Simon the Magician, Basilides, Cerinthus and many others. It is also possible to infer what views they held from books two to five, in which Irenaeus challenges the 'heretics' with many arguments. Irenaeus wrote in Greek, but a good deal of this version has been lost. However, his work has been preserved in a Latin translation, and partly in a translation into Armenian.

Tertullian is another church father worth mentioning. He lived in Carthage in the Roman province of Africa, present-day Tunisia. Around 193 he had become a Christian, but he did not stay in the catholic church. In 208 he left this church to join the movement of the 'New Prophecy', also called Montanism. This movement was disseminated from Phrygia in Asia Minor by Montanus, who was supported by two prophetesses. They attached great importance to the gift of prophecy and expected a speedy coming of the kingdom of God. Tertullian valued the great emphasis on a holy life in this movement: he thought the catholic authorities too lax over penance after serious sin. He wrote books in Latin against the gnostics both in his catholic and his Montanist period. Some titles are: *The Prescription of Heretics, Against Hermogenes, Against the Valentinians, The Resurrection of the Dead*. Although Tertullian does not quote gnostic views as extensively as Irenaeus, his books do contain important information about the gnostics.

Third, Hippolytus needs to be mentioned. At the beginning of the third century he was a priest of the church in Rome, but in 217 he came into conflict there with the then bishop Callixtus. The conflict – as in the case of Tertullian previously – was over the relatively mild rules of the church about sin, penance and forgiveness. As a result of this, Hippolytus became bishop or president of a separate, stricter community. Between 222 and 235 (the year of his death) he wrote a work in ten books under the title *Refutation of all Heresies*. In it, like Irenaeus, he discussed many gnostic writings and quoted from them. The work was written in Greek and has not been preserved in its entirety. There is only one known manuscript which contains the books about the gnostics; this dates from the fourteenth century and is of bad quality.

The three church fathers discussed so far were active in the

Western part of the Roman church. The first person of importance from the Eastern part of the empire among those who were intensively concerned with gnosticism is Clement of Alexandria. He gave instruction in the Christian religion in that city. In the period between 193 and the beginning of the third century he wrote a work in Greek in seven books with the title *Stromateis* (literally 'Carpets'). In it he gives a number of quotations from gnostic teachers like Basilides, his son Isidorus, Valentinus, Carpocrates and Heracleon. A valuable summary which Clement made of a work by the Valentinian Theodotus has also been preserved. Although Clement regarded the gnostics as heretics, some of his views were related to theirs. His own emphasis on the gnosis which is to be learned in the catholic church is striking. He himself also called advanced Christians gnostics, by which he meant that church membership is not just about faith but also about a deeper insight, gnosis. These works have been preserved primarily in a Greek manuscript from the eleventh century.

Like Clement, Origen too was originally active in Alexandria as a teacher in the Christian religion. Around 230, however, he came into conflict with his bishop Demetrius, because Demetrius could not accept his daring philosophical expositions of the Christian faith. He was excommunicated by a synod in Alexandria, but was able to continue his work at Caesarea in Palestine, as an ordained priest and under the supervision of the bishop there. Although Origen too, like Clement, sometimes shows an affinity with the 'heretical' gnostics, he emphatically distances himself from them. He mentions the gnostics regularly in his extensive work, but always in a critical sense. Origen's *Commentary on the Gospel of John* is very valuable, although it has not been preserved in its entirety. In it he offers a number of quotations from the gnostic commentary which the Valentinian Heracleon had written on this Gospel earlier. His work *Against Celsus*, in which he deals with the mockery and criticism by a philosopher of this name, also contains some gnostic fragments. These works have been handed down in Greek in various mediaeval manuscripts.

Epiphanius of Salamis is the last figure worth mentioning in this context. After being head of a monastery in Palestine which he founded for about thirty years, in 367 he became bishop of Salamis on Cyprus. Around ten years later he completed his extensive work *Panarion*, which means 'breadbasket' or – according to his own explanation – 'medicine chest'. In it he describes (in Greek) eighty philosophies and heresies which he regarded as poisonous, and for which he wanted to provide cures. His descriptions of the eighty tendencies vary considerably in length and reliability. For the gnostics he often resorts to Irenaeus and Hippolytus, but he also regularly offers other valuable information about them, and sometimes – at least to go by his own words – he draws on personal experience. Epiphanius' *Panarion* has been handed down in some Greek manuscripts from the Middle Ages.

3. The structure of this book

This book contains an *introduction* to the gnosticism which appears in early Christianity or is connected with it; thus it does not provide a comprehensive treatment of this subject. There are so many and varied testimonies to gnosticism in late antiquity that it would be impossible to discuss them all within the scope of this book. So instead of striving for completeness, I shall discuss what in my view is a representative selection of ancient gnosis. An important emphasis in this study is the background and origin of gnosticism. Thus I shall especially try to answer the question: Where does this phenomenon come from?

I have set myself the aim of writing this book like a detective. Of course the comparison falls short, but what I mean is this. I shall try to make the reader gradually familiar with the topics and ingredients of gnosticism without directly explaining where all the different elements come from. In this way I hope to arouse curiosity and a sense of discovery; while reading, there is always more to discover. So my intention is for the attentive reader slowly to track down the identity of gnosis and to conclude where it comes from. Those who have gained insights into the background and origin of gnosticism can also apply this knowledge to gnostic texts which are not discussed here.

By way of a first orientation Part I – Chapters 2, 3, and 4 – contains a relatively long discussion of a limited number of witnesses from gnosticism. After that, in Part II – in Chapters 5–8 – I investigate the question of the religious and philosophical backgrounds to gnosticism. In Part III – in Chapter 9 – I bring the texts discussed so far together and engage in a more detailed discussion of terms like 'gnosis' and 'gnosticism'. This chapter as it were unravels the question what gnosticism is about. In it I set out systematically where the search of gnosticism has led me, and with me the reader.

For the sake of clarity, Chapters 2 to 9 are based on a limited number of gnostic witnesses. However, so as not to keep this 'introduction to gnosticism' all too limited, I broaden the horizons in Chapters 10 and 11. In them some further persons and texts which are gnostic or called gnostic or are akin to gnosticism are discussed, but less extensively than those in Part I. A concluding Part IV – Chapters 12 and 13 – is about the relationship between old 'catholic' Christianity and gnosticism. Also in the light of the present-day interest in ancient gnosticism, in it I shall try there to make an assessment of this phenomenon.

Finally, a comment on the use of capitals. This book is about all kinds of gods and a great many heavenly and divine powers. It is usual to write the god of the Bible with a capital letter, God. It is also customary to write god with a small letter in the case of deities from classical antiquity. Since in gnosticism there is such an intensive interaction between the Bible and late antiquity, it would often be difficult and arbitrary to distinguish between God and god. I have therefore decided to be generous in the distribution of capital letters, although I am not strictly consistent. This applies to 'God'; the same question arises with terms like Creator, Mother, Father, Spirit and so on. Here too I usually write capitals, as in other designations of heavenly powers. However, I do not pretend to be completely consistent. The languages in which the sources studied were written (Hebrew, Greek, Latin, Coptic, Syriac) do not know the problem; in them people did not use capitals.

2

Irenaeus on the origin of the heresies

In Chapter 1 it proved that from the second century of our era onwards, a number of testimonies are known from and about groups which are now known as gnostic. This raises all kinds of questions. From where or from whom do their views come? Precisely what was the content of the earliest gnosis?

Irenaeus of Lyons, around the year 180, also raises the question of the 'source and root' of the heresies.[1] The term heresies (in Latin *haereses*) certainly contains a value judgment, but we should not be surprised at that in a catholic bishop like Irenaeus. He is then referring to those groups which he also calls gnostics.

He answers his question with a reference to Simon the Magician. Simon occurs in the New Testament, in Acts 8.9–24. Irenaeus indicates that there were still followers of this Simon in his time, and he gives a short sketch of their belief systems, in other words, gnosis. Tertullian, Hippolytus and Epiphanius also write about Simon and the views of his later followers. Their facts are based on those of Irenaeus, supplement them and also differ from them.

In Irenaeus's information about Simon we can recognize a very simple – and thus probably early – doctrine of redemption. Therefore I shall begin to discuss the various currents which are called gnostic with this Simon and the group that appealed to him in the second century. Here I shall keep primarily to what Irenaeus says, but I will sometimes also refer to the other church fathers.[2] After that I shall take a brief look at Menander of Antioch, who is named by Irenaeus as Simon's successor.

1. *Simon the magician*

1.1. *Traditions about Simon the magician*

According to the biblical book of the Acts of the Apostles, Simon was renowned in Samaria for his magic. He had many admirers among the Samaritans and they called him the 'great power of God'. Thus they regarded him as a man of God who could do miracles by divine inspiration. The author tells of this Simon when he describes how Philip, a prominent member of the earliest Christian community in Jerusalem,[3] came to Samaria and called on the Samaritans to believe in Jesus Christ. The consequence was that many of them listened to him. Simon saw this and was impressed by the miracles that Philip did. He too came to believe and was baptized. Soon afterwards, according to this report, the apostles Peter and John came from Jerusalem to lay hands on those who had been baptized so that they should receive the holy Spirit. Simon was also impressed by this. Thereupon he offered money to Peter and John in exchange for authority from them also to be able to convey the holy Spirit by the laying on of hands. Simon was then unmasked by Peter as an insincere convert with whom things would go wrong. According to Acts, Simon thereupon asked Peter to pray for him. We are not told the sequel. These events could have taken place around the year 40.

In this account there is no trace of any form of gnosticism. The first beginnings of this in connection with Simon can only be found in the second century, with Justin Martyr, who like Simon came from Samaria. Among other of his works we know of two apologies for the Christian faith which he wrote around the middle of the second century. In the First Apology he reports that in the time of the emperor Claudius (who reigned from 41–54) Simon had performed all kinds of magic arts in Rome and was worshipped as divine. Justin also relates that almost all Samaritans recognize and worship Simon as the highest (literally first) God. He adds that one Helen, a former prostitute, had accompanied Simon, and that she had been called his 'First Thought' by the Samaritans.[4]

This last fact – and its gnostic tenor – is understandable only in Irenaeus.[5] Irenaeus reports that Simon had redeemed this prostitute Helen in the Phoenician city of Tyre. Simon himself was said to be an incarnation of the highest God, who thought that in this Helen he could recognize his 'First Thought', the 'Mother of all things', or 'Mother of all'. Irenaeus then relates in brief the myth which underlies this story. This myth runs as follows.

In the beginning the highest God, the Father, had the thought of creating angels and archangels. This 'First Thought' sprang from him, descended to lower regions, and there brought forth angels and powers. Tertullian explains that here she was anticipating the purpose of the Father; apparently she went to work to some degree of her own accord and in a sense she was disobedient.[6]

These angels and powers then created the world. However, they could not accept that they were descended from someone else. Out of envy of the 'First Thought' which had brought them forth, they took her prisoner and shut her up in a human body. She was doomed century after century to move from one woman's body to another. This 'First Thought' was reincarnated, for example, in Helen, the woman who was the occasion for the Trojan War. (Helen was the wife of the king of Sparta, but she was abducted by Paris, the son of the king of Troy. Since the Trojans were not prepared to return Helen, the Greeks declared war on Troy.) When the poet Stesichorus insulted her (probably he had asserted that she had gone with Paris of her own free will), he was struck blind as a punishment, but when he withdrew his insult he regained his sight.

In all her reincarnations the 'First Thought' of the Father was humiliated and shamed. Finally she lived as a prostitute in a brothel in Tyre. She was the 'lost sheep' of the Gospel. In the meantime these angels and powers who governed the world had no idea of the existence of the highest God, the Father.

Then the highest God himself came to free the 'First Thought' from her fetters. He descended, but he did not want to redeem her alone. Because the angels had governed the world badly, all human beings had had to suffer under them, and therefore the highest God also came to offer redemption to human beings generally and to improve their state. For them this redemption consisted in the knowledge of the highest God himself.[7]

In order to descend to the world unnoticed, he made his appearance like that of the angels, forces and powers. (To explain: in this way he could pass unhindered through the higher spheres and regions over which they had power.[8]) When he arrived on earth he made himself like human beings and thus appeared as a human being, although he was not one. It seemed as if he had suffered in Judaea, but in reality he had not.

The followers of Simon – Irenaeus calls them 'Simonians' – thus regarded Simon as the manifestation of the highest God, who had revealed the true knowledge to humankind. But they did not think that the truth could be found only in Simon. They believed that the highest God had appeared to the Jews as the Son, to the Samaritans as the Father, and that he had come to the other peoples as the holy Spirit. According to them, it did not matter to the Father who is above all things what people called him. However, the Simonians asserted that the Old Testament prophets had not been inspired by the highest God, but by the angels who had created the world. These angels had led humankind into slavery with all kinds of arbitrary commandments. However, Simon had promised to destroy this world and to free his followers from the power of the angels.

The Simonians thought that people could not be redeemed by doing 'righteous works', but only by Simon's grace. Those who had set their hope on Simon and Helen would also be free to do what they wanted. Moreover Irenaeus accused the 'priests' who initiated others into this knowledge of leading loose lives. He writes that they engaged in magical practices like driving out evil spirits and uttering adjurations and magical spells. Finally, Irenaeus mentions that the Simonians had an image of Simon in the form of the Greek God Zeus and an image of Helen in the form of Zeus's daughter Athene, and that they also worshipped these images.

Although Irenaeus doubtless accepted that this myth and 'knowledge' of it had been handed down by Simon the Magician himself, this is improbable. After all, Irenaeus was writing more than a century after Simon, and it is very questionable whether at that time he had new historically accurate information about him.[9] Because Justin Martyr already mentions the later myth of Simon and Helen in a nutshell, around 150, we are to assume that this came into being in the first half of the second century; perhaps already around 100. Accordingly, Irenaeus wrongly assumed that these facts were historically correct.

1.2. *Analysis and interpretation of the myth of Simon and Helen*

1.2.1. *The highest God descends to earth*

In this myth Simon emerges as someone who wants to make people see how the world is made and what life on earth is worth. According to this myth there is a highest God, but he did not create the world. This God wanted to create only angels and archangels and to do this by means of his 'First Thought', who is presented as a separate spiritual figure. Moreover she is called the Mother of all things or the Mother of all. So we can see that according to the Simonians the highest God, the Father, has a female form in or beside himself.

However, probably something already went wrong in the way in which the First Thought created the angels and the powers: after springing from the Father she had produced them too much in accordance with her own insight. If this interpretation is right, then the creation of the world by these angels also stands in a bad light. In any case these angels were no use because they were jealous. They could not accept that there was a heavenly power above them, namely the First Thought, the Mother of all, and therefore took her prisoner. They shackled her to a human body, or more precisely to a whole series of female bodies, in which time and again she had to be reincarnated.

At least three things are to be inferred from this. First, the highest God is not directly involved in the creation of the world because the angelic powers were responsible for this. Secondly, these angels do not know about the existence of the highest God. So there is a gulf or a division between the highest God on the one hand and the angelic powers and their world on the other. Thirdly, something that has sprung from the highest God, called his First Thought, has got on the wrong side of the gulf because contrary to her destiny she has got mixed up with earthly bodies. This indicates that life on earth in a human body has no positive purpose, but rather is a tragic fate that comes about from a fall and an imprisonment. Nevertheless, it also emerges from this that an element of the highest God can still be present in a human body.

Although the highest God is not responsible for the creation of this world and for earthly life, he has mercy on his First Thought which is held fast in it. But he also has mercy on human beings generally. From this it emerges that there is an affinity between the fate of the First Thought and that of humankind. Thus the highest God descends and takes the form of a human being in Simon of Samaria. However, it can be inferred from Irenaeus' words about the apparent suffering of this God in Judaea that the Simonians recognized that the highest God had also descended in Jesus. It is testified that he suffered on a cross near Jerusalem – thus in Judaea – and died. Belief in a multiple revelation of the highest God is also expressed in the view that he appeared to the Jews as the Son and the Samaritans as the Father, and that he has come to the other peoples as the holy Spirit.

However, the myth is above all about the manifestation of the highest God in the Samaritan Simon. His redemption of the prostitute Helen from a brothel in Tyre is the symbol of human redemption. He makes her true identity known to her. Since then she has been reunited with the God from whom she originally came. Simon and Helen travel round together as an eloquent testimony that the divine which is imprisoned in a human body can be touched by the grace of true knowledge and communion with the highest God, and can be redeemed again.

1.2.2. Relation to the Old Testament

A notable aspect of the Simonian myth is that the Old Testament prophets were not inspired by the highest God but by the lower angels who were responsible for the creation of the world. Thus the Simonians did not agree with the Old Testament view that the Lord (Yahweh) is the most high God who created heaven and earth. They also had a very negative view of the commandments that the angelic powers had instituted, because according to them these commandments led people into slavery.

From the fact that the Simonians felt compelled to adopt a standpoint on the Old Testament, it seems that this was an important book for those around them. From what Irenaeus says, we can infer that the Simonians put the Lord and God of Israel among the lower angelic powers that they abhorred.

1.2.3. Relation to the New Testament

It is striking that this myth has some superficial links with the writings which later came to be called the New Testament. They constantly treat or interpret New Testament facts in a distinctive way. At least four examples of this can be given.

First, that the highest God takes human form and that it is thought that he suffered in Judaea suggests the divine Word that has been made flesh in Jesus (John 1.14) and Jesus' crucifixion. However, there are also differences: according to the New Testament it is not God the Father himself who becomes man, while according to the myth, the highest God did not really become man and did not really suffer.[10] This view of the incarnation and the suffering of the highest God is called 'docetic', which means 'apparent'.[11]

Secondly, the view that the highest God appeared to the Jews as the Son, to the Samaritans as the Father and has come to other peoples as the holy Spirit is clearly an interpretation of Christian belief in God the Father, the Son and the holy Spirit.

Thirdly: a clear use of the New Testament comes to light when the prostitute Helen is called the lost sheep. However, Jesus' parable of the lost sheep in Luke 15.3–7 is not set in this mythical context.

Fourthly, the Simonians thought that the Old Testament commandments led to slavery and that one could not be redeemed by doing 'righteous works' but only through Simon's grace. This suggests the letters of Paul. Paul too associated the Old Testament with slavery.[12] In his view one is not justified by the 'works of the law' but only through faith in Jesus Christ: 'through grace you are redeemed, through faith'.[13] Thus the Simonian myth also seems to be inspired by the letters of Paul, but it is clear that the words which are apparently derived from this are put in another context.

So we can see that the adherents to this myth take a negative stance over the Old Testament and that they offer their own interpretation of the New Testament.

1.2.4. *Relations with Greek antiquity*

Apart from this negative or alternative use of the Old and New Testaments, other, Greek, elements occur in this myth. To begin with the end of Irenaeus' rendering: there it is evident that Simon and Helen are also worshipped as Zeus and Athene. This corresponds to the beginning of the myth, in which a 'First Thought' detached itself from the highest God. According to Greek mythology Athene sprang straight from Zeus' head. Therefore in later interpretations Athene was called Zeus' mind or even his 'First Thought'.[14]

Secondly, according to the myth of the Simonians the First Thought was taken prisoner and shut up in a series of human bodies. This suggests the philosophy of Plato (450–347 BCE), which in turn goes back to other philosophers before him. In Plato's dialogues it is said that the body is a prison for the soul. The soul has to escape from it and return to the higher world from which it came. But if a soul has not lived a pious and virtuous human life, then it must first be reincarnated in another body, until it is completely purified.[15]

A third Greek element in the myth of Simon and Helen emerges when Helen is identified with the woman over whom the Trojan War began. It was a well-known fact, related by Plato among others, that the Greek poet Stesichorus withdrew his initial censure of Helen.[16]

In Chapter 9 I shall return to other Greek elements in this myth. However, it is already sufficiently clear from these three examples that the Simonians not only took up facts from the New Testament, but at least as easily referred back to Greek antiquity. Since they rejected the Old Testament, for them the Greek myths and philosophy seem to have occupied the place that the Old Testament took in the Christian church.

1.2.5. The redemptive power of the myth of Simon and Helen

At the end of this analysis and interpretation of the myth of Simon and Helen I shall go briefly into some essential questions. What was this myth essentially about? What does it express in depth? Why did people have faith in such a story and discover their salvation in it?

My answer to these questions is only provisional at this stage and later I will develop it more broadly. The aim of my provisional answer to these questions is to make it clear from the beginning how myths like that of Simon and Helen are relevant to existential questions.

The traditional religions taught that there were one or more gods who had created this earth and who were concerned for human beings on earth. So as a mortal one could call on this god or these gods for help and redemption. Not everyone will have experienced that their prayers – and sacrifices – achieved anything. The effects of fate like sickness, oppression, war, death and sorrow continued. People could feel inwardly or physically unclean and polluted. God or the gods seemed far away from all this. The religion of the ancestors did not satisfy in every respect.

Against the background of this experience a group like the Simonians taught that this world was not created by a good God but by lower, jealous angels; that this world was therefore not meant to come into being as it is; that human life on earth was the consequence of a fall from on high and therefore was often tragic. Hence the misery.

So was there any possibility of escaping it? Yes, thank God. There is a true highest God, high above this world, who cannot be made responsible for the misery in this world. In his mercy this God himself descended to earth to make himself known to those who despite everything are related to him. He wills to redeem them from the hopeless cycle of life on earth. This world should cease to exist, but by means of messengers the highest God reveals the 'knowledge' which is needed in order to be united with him and to be redeemed from misery. So these messengers point the way to God and indicate what in human beings is akin to God: the divine in human beings. Anyone who has learned to know this gnosis lives in a different way. Such a person is already redeemed at depth.

The Simonians associated this knowledge with the Samaritan Simon, who was already revered in Samaria and elsewhere – as in Rome. The Simonians thought that they had still deeper knowledge about Simon: he had not been just a magician or a divine man; no, the highest God himself had descended on him. The redemption of Helen from the brothel essentially indicates the redemption of human beings from a sordid life without insight. One's soiled soul could be redeemed and reunited with the true God. People were attracted by this message. This redemption gave earthy life a new splendour.

2. *Menander of Antioch*

After his discussion of Simon the Magician and the Simonians Irenaeus briefly discusses one Menander, also a Samaritan, as Simon's successor.[17] We learn from Justin that this Menander was active in Antioch, where he did magic. According to Irenaeus's account he proclaimed that there was a 'First Power' who was unknown to everyone. Like the Simonians, Menander taught that the world had been created by angels, and that the angels had been brought forth through the 'Thought'. Menander saw himself as the Redeemer who had been sent from the invisible world for the redemption of human beings. With the help of magic – according to Irenaeus – he provided the knowledge that was necessary to overcome the angels who had created the world. Anyone who as his disciple had undergone 'baptism in him' received the resurrection and could not die again. Such a person would never grow old and had become immortal.

It is possible that Irenaeus's brief account of Menander's teaching is to some degree a caricature. Moreover it is improbable that with his teaching this Menander really built on the teaching of Simon himself. Certainly we can recognize in this rough sketch a doctrine of redemption which is akin to the myth of Simon, seems even simpler and is perhaps also older. Menander taught about an unknown highest God who is not Creator of the world, and about his 'Thought' which produced angels who then created the word. That their rule of the world was not at all pleasant is evident from the purpose of Menander's 'knowledge', namely for human beings to learn to win the victory over angels.

At least according to Irenaeus, Menander regarded himself as the Redeemer who had been sent from heaven. This differs from the myth of Simon, who is presented as an incarnation in which the highest God himself had descended. Certainly Menander, as the Redeemer sent from heaven, resembles Jesus as he is described in the Gospel of John. Similarly, there is apparently an agreement between the immortality promised by Menander and the 'eternal life' in the preaching of Jesus according to the Gospel of John.[18] However, Menander's proclamation of an immortal life on earth bears witness to a remarkable optimism about the conquest of death and of the angelic powers. The element that those baptized by Menander would never grow old could also be mockery on the part of Irenaeus, but that they are baptized 'in him' again suggests baptism 'in Christ'.[19]

It is evident from the emphasis on the victory over the angelic powers and the obtaining of immortality that Menander wanted to offer a solution to the suffering and threat of death which are characteristic of earthly life. The fact that there is mention of baptism and of 'magical' practices indicates communal worship. Possibly here we are on the track of one of the earliest forms of 'heretical' Gnosticism which can be traced, and which can be put at the end of the first century. Some agreements with belief in Jesus Christ are striking here. However, Irenaeus does not make it clear whether Menander was familiar with the Christian faith or whether he offered himself as a better alternative to Jesus Christ.

3. Irenaeus, gnostics and gnosis

After his discussion of Simon and Menander, Irenaeus discusses a large number of other 'heretics'. For example he describes Satornilus, Carpocrates, Cerinthus, the Ebionites, Nicolaus, Cerdo, Marcion and the Ophites; and before Simon he had discussed extensively the teaching of Ptolemaeus from the school of Valentinus. Irenaeus thinks that the views of all these 'heretics' are to be derived from Simon and Menander. But he can also say that a large number of 'gnostics' had come from the Simonians.[20] For the moment I will simply remark that Irenaeus does not explicitly call Simon and Menander 'gnostics', but that he does refer to the 'knowledge' – in other words gnosis – that they teach.

A characteristic of their gnosis is a division or dualism

between the highest God and the created world. The highest God is not the Creator of the world. Lower angelic powers are responsible for the creation and government of the world; they emerged from a female figure who had detached herself from the highest God.

Life in this world is anything but pleasant, and although the highest God is not responsible for it, he does take the initiative in the redemption of human beings in the world. He himself descends, as in the myth of Simon, or he sends a Redeemer, the role which Menander saw himself as playing. Such messengers of the most high God make known the gnosis which offers insight into the true state of things and which is necessary for finding spiritual redemption in the difficulties of earthly life.

3

A sermon from the
Nag Hammadi books

The two examples of gnosis in the previous chapter were taken from the descriptions of Irenaeus and some other church fathers. The disadvantage of this introduction could be that these models are based on authors who disputed this gnosis. This raises the question how reliable their information is. Therefore it is important to discuss a writing from the Nag Hammadi collection which shows a striking affinity to the myth of Simon and Helen. Its title is The Exegesis (or Interpretation) on the Soul. This writing, which relates the vicissitudes of the soul, presumably comes from the second century.[1] I shall first give a summary of it and then compare it with the myth of Simon and Helen.

1. The Exegesis on the Soul

This sermon on the soul begins by saying that the soul is feminine by nature and has a womb. After this introduction the man or woman who is speaking here begins with the state in which the soul still was with the Father. She was then virgin and androgynous; this last means that she was both male and female. But when the soul fell from the house of the Father down into a female body, she fell into the hands of robbers who dishonoured her and abused her. Thus she lost her virginity. She gave herself to whoever wanted her and thought that everyone was her consort; thus she lived as a prostitute (127–128).

She repented, but did not immediately succeed in breaking off her intercourse with men; this continued for a long time. The children that she bore to them were dumb, blind, sickly and feeble-minded (128).

When the Father sees that the soul has repented and that she is beginning to call on his name and asking for redemption, then, in the author's view, he will have mercy on her. In connection with the prostitution in which the soul is engaged, he (or she) cites some passages from the Old Testament prophets in which Israel is compared with a woman who has often been unfaithful to her husband, the Lord.[2] The author recalls that the apostles of the Redeemer, too, had warned against prostitution, both in a physical and in a spiritual sense.[3] It is explained that when a soul comes to repentance, the Father turns her womb, which was external, back inwards again.[4] The soul then receives her own identity back and is purified and baptized (128–132).

Because as a woman she cannot produce children alone, the Father has sent her consort to her from heaven. This consort is at the same time her firstborn brother. She had been bound to him in the beginning, when she was still in the Father's house. The soul looked to him, although she did not know him because she no longer remembered the Father's house. But the bridegroom came, and they united in the bridal chamber – which is emphatically not a reference to fleshly marriage. According to the narrator this spiritual union is meant when it is said of the first man and the first woman 'they shall become one flesh'.[5] The seed that the soul received from this bridegroom was the Spirit which makes alive,[6] and so she brought forth good children. As a testimony to this conversion the narrator cites Psalm 45, which says that the bride must forget her people and her father's house. To explain this, he draws a distinction between the house of her earthly father, where things went badly with her, and her Father in heaven, whom she must remember. He also refers to Abraham, who had to depart from his father's house (132–133).[7]

The soul, who is as she was originally, experiences resurrection from the dead; she ascends to the Father and is born again, as the prophet bore witness.[8] She is not redeemed by practising asceticism or by a special proficiency or by written instruction, but only by the grace of God.[9] Therefore the Redeemer exclaimed: 'No one can come to me unless my Father draws him and brings him to me; and I myself will raise him up on the last day' (134–135).[10]

The author calls on us to pray to the Father with all our soul and to confess our sins. Again he cites the Old and the New Testaments. Moreover at the end of his argument he refers to the poet Homer, who described how Odysseus longed to return home. He also quotes from the Odyssey words of Helen, who in Troy asserts that she wants to go home and regrets that she has left her daughter and husband.[11] The end of this sermon runs: 'If we repent, truly God will heed us, he who is long suffering and abundantly merciful, to whom is the glory for ever and ever. Amen' (135–137).

2. The Exegesis on the Soul compared with 'Simon and Helen'

The affinity between the myth of Simon and Helen and the Exegesis on the Soul which has already been mentioned does not go so far that Simon of Samaria appears again in this writing. Nor is Simon's partner Helen mentioned, though words of repentance are cited from Helen who remained in Troy. (Where we expect the name Helen the manuscript is damaged, but it is virtually certain that 'Helen' must be supplied here.) Despite this lack of similarity on the surface, though, the role which the soul occupies in this 'Exegesis' does seem very like the fate of the First Thought from the myth of Simon and Helen. In both cases there is an expulsion from the presence of the Father on high and an imprisonment or fall in a female body on earth, where the First Thought, and then the soul, falls prey to prostitution. Both the First Thought and the soul are redeemed in this earthly life, although the figure of the

Redeemer is not the same. Another agreement is that the redemption is described in sexual terms: the female figure unites with her original male partner from heaven. In both testimonies it is said that the redemption is not to be earned by human achievements but is attributable only to grace.

There are also differences, apart from the deviations I have already indicated. Here we must realize that the differences relate not only to the content but also to the form of the tradition. The myth of Simon and Helen is known only in brief renderings by some critical church fathers, while the 'Exegesis on the Soul' is a kind of sermon in narrative form, which is delivered with verve by someone who believes in it.

A first difference in content is that this sermon, unlike the myth, does not contain an exposition of the creation of the world by lower angelic powers. The 'robbers', like the angels, lead the soul to prostitution, but they are not identified more closely.

A second difference from the Simonian myth is that in the Exegesis on the Soul the Old Testament is regularly cited with approval. The Old Testament prophets are not connected with the lower angelic powers as in the myth of the Simonians. Nevertheless, the Father from whom the soul has removed herself is not called the Creator. It is not explained who has created the world.

A third difference is that in the Exegesis on the Soul the New Testament is cited much more often than in the myth of Simon and Helen – at least in Irenaeus' brief summary.

Fourthly, as I have already pointed out, the redeemer figures are presented differently. In the myth, the historical figures of Simon and, in view of the reference to the crucifixion in Judaea, also Jesus, play this role. In the Exegesis on the Soul it remains unclear in what form the bridegroom, who at the same time is the older brother of the soul, comes to her. Although sayings of Jesus are cited and the speaker is then called the Redeemer, he is not identified with the bridegroom. There is no suggestion that the bridegroom has appeared as Redeemer in a human being of flesh and blood; he can best be compared with the Holy Spirit as this is mentioned in the myth of Simon and Helen.

Fifthly, in contrast to the myth of Simon and Helen, the term 'knowledge' does not play any significant role in the Exegesis on the Soul. However, this sermon is about the 'recollection' of the house of the Father, and 'repentance' or conversion are required as a condition of redemption.

Sixthly, Irenaeus writes that after their redemption the Simonians could do what they wanted and accused them of loose living. Nothing of this appears in the Exegesis on the Soul.

3. *The Exegesis on the Soul, gnosis and Christianity*

Some points need to be developed further. In this sermon on the fate of the soul the term 'knowledge' – or 'gnosis' – does not play a central role. In connection with this all that is said of the soul is that she no longer knew the bridegroom, and that when the bridegroom did unite with her again, she gradually came to know him. This figure of the bridegroom raises the question what image of God the author of the Exegesis on the Soul had. Is the Father, who sends the bridegroom and brother of the soul for her redemption, at the same time the Creator and governor of the world? Did this Father thus want life on earth? And what is the significance of the fact that no connection is made between the bridegroom of the soul and Jesus as Redeemer?

In connection with the image of God it is perhaps important that the author speaks in passing, on the basis of Psalm 45, of an earthly father with whom the soul had a bad time and whom she therefore has to leave. There is then also a reference to Abraham who similarly has to leave his father's house. By this earthly father the author could be referring to the God of the world, whom he would then – if this interpretation is correct – be distinguishing from the Father in heaven.[12] In the past this distinction has usually been called 'gnostic'. However, it is also possible to regard the earthly father as a symbol of all unwanted ties on earth from which the soul can be redeemed. It is then striking that the term 'robbers' that is used for the powers which reduce the soul to prostitution is elsewhere a term used to denote the angelic powers of the lower Creator.[13]

There is also, as I have said, the striking point that Jesus is cited and then the Redeemer is mentioned, though he is not identified with the bridegroom. This gives the impression that the story of a heavenly bridegroom and redeemer was already in existence, and that here some words of Jesus and his apostles are quoted by way of a Christian adaptation. However, this adaptation – or Christianization – is not so developed that the bridegroom is called Jesus Christ.

It can be inferred from this that this sermon does not only – or even primarily – have a biblical background. Without going into other sources, I shall anticipate by referring to a relevant passage in the Neo-Platonic philosopher Plotinus who lived from 204 to 270. He wrote:

> The soul then in her natural state is in love with God and wants to be united with him; it is like the noble love of a girl [virgin] for her noble father. But when the soul has come into the world of becoming and is deceived, so to say, by the blandishments of her suitors, she changes, bereft of her father, to a mortal love and is shamed; but again she comes to hate her shames here below, and purifies herself of the things of this world and sets herself on the way to her father and fares well.[14]

Thus the Exegesis on the Soul seems to be related to the myth of Simon and Helen, but also to the Platonic philosophy of this time. The many quotations from the Old and New Testaments indicate that these books were authoritative for the author and that he was addressing Christians. From the quotations from Homer it appears that he did not forget Greek culture either.

4

Refinements of the gnostic myth

The nucleus of the view of the spiritual redemption of humankind according to Menander, the Simonians and the Exegesis on the Soul is relatively simple. It is about a highest God who is distinguished from the lower powers which are responsible for the creation of the material world, or at least for the misfortune of the soul on earth. The cause of the alienation and brokenness of human life on earth lies in a fall from on high. At the same time this means that human beings are deep down akin to the highest God. However, they need a redeemer to be told of this and to rediscover the original unity.

A number of variations and refinements of this simple doctrine of redemption were made in the second century. Two of them will be discussed in this chapter. First, Satornilus of Antioch, whose views have been handed down briefly by some church fathers. Then follows a discussion of the Secret Book of John, which is extant in various Coptic versions. Finally, I shall give some examples of the phenomenon of the 'passwords' which the soul needs for her final redemption.

1. Satornilus of Antioch

1.1. The myth of Satornilus

Irenaeus is the first person to mention Satornilus of Antioch (the Latin version of his name is Saturninus). This part of Irenaeus's work has been handed down in a Latin translation; however, because his text about Satornilus is cited in Greek by Hippolytus, the original version has been preserved.[1] Irenaeus mentions Satornilus in the same breath as Basilides of Alexandria and explains that the teachings of these two derive from Simon the Magician and Menander. This is improbable in the case of Simon the Magician, although Satornilus can be dependent on the views of the Simonians; however, the reference to Menander could be correct. This would mean – also in view of the fact that he is mentioned alongside Basilides – that Satornilus' appearance can be dated at the beginning of the second century.

According to Satornilus there is one Father who is unknown to all and who has created the angels, archangels, forces and powers. Seven of the angels created the world and all that is in it, including human beings. The creation of humankind was done in this way. A shining image of the highest 'authority' – this clearly means the Father – appeared to the angels. Because this image immediately disappeared on high again, the angels could not grasp it. They then had an idea: 'Let us make a human being after the image and the likeness' (cf. Gen. 1.26). But when they had made a human being, it could not stand upright and continued to wriggle like a worm. The 'power from on high' – clearly the Father – then had compassion on the human being who had been created after his likeness, and sent a spark of light. As a result of this the human being stood upright and received life. After his death this spark of life rises to that to which it is akin and the rest of the human being – his body – decays into corruption.

Satornilus thought that the figure of the Redeemer is unbegotten and incorporeal and has no form, but has nevertheless shown itself in the appearance of a human being. This means that he has 'seemingly' shown himself as a human being.

According to Satornilus, the God of the Jews was one of the created angels. He also calls them 'rulers', in Greek *archontes*. Since the unknown Father planned to destroy all these archons,[2] Christ came to destroy the God of the Jews and to bring redemption to whoever trusted in him; redemption comes to those who have the spark of life in them. Satornilus distinguished between two sorts of human beings. There are the bad who have allowed themselves to be helped by the demons. Here Irenaeus indicates that according to Satornilus, marriage and the procreation of children are inspired by Satan. However, the Redeemer has come to destroy the bad human beings and the demons. But there are also good human beings, those who have received the divine spark of life and have been redeemed by the Redeemer. They live a chaste and austere life and most of them abstain from meat.

Satornilus' view of the Old Testament prophets was that these are partly inspired by the angels who created the world and partly by Satan. Satan is one of the angels, but he is an opponent of the angels who created the world and is most of all an opponent of the God of the Jews. Thus Irenaeus's account.

1.2. Notes on the myth of Satornilus

There now follow some comments on this teaching of Satornilus, on the presupposition that the summary which Irenaeus made of it – and which is followed by other church fathers – is more or less correct. In Part II I shall go in more detail into the biblical and philosophical elements of such myths (which are called gnostic). For the moment I shall limit myself on this background and offer above all a comparison of the views of Menander and the Simonians.

The affinity of this teaching of Satornilus with that of Menander and the Simonians is immediately obvious. Satornilus, too, proclaims an unknown highest God, the Father, who did not create the material world, far less human beings. Certainly he created 'angels, archangels, forces and powers'. But the figure of the 'First Thought' is missing in Satornilus; according to him the unknown Father created the angelic powers without the intervention of another figure.

In the case of Satornilus it is striking that he has introduced a number of distinctions between various angelic powers which we did not meet in this form in Menander and the

Simonians. Certainly the terms 'angels, archangels, forces and powers' occurred with the Simonians, but what is new is that the material world and human beings are created by *seven* angels, of whom the God of the Jews is one. We can see a connection here with the Jewish notion that there were seven archangels.[3] In Jewish terminology these angels are called archons or 'rulers'. It is striking that the other six angels out of these seven are not identified – at least in Irenaeus's account. It seems to follow from this that Satornilus was concerned to offer a distinctive interpretation of the Old Testament. This is confirmed by the mention of Satan as an angel who turned against the creator angels, but especially against the God of the Jews. Satornilus's view of the Old Testament is that it is partly inspired by the creator angels and partly by Satan. This goes further than the view of the Simonians, who thought that the Old Testament was inspired only by the creator angels.

The motif that the Father appeared briefly to the seven creator angels is also new. They then tried to create the human being in the image of this appearance and in so doing used words from Gen. 1.26.[4] Thus it seems that according to Satornilus the highest God in a sense had human form, or at least could appear in the form of a human being.

However, the angels only partly succeed in creating a human being. Thereupon the Father has mercy on this pitiable worm and sends him the spark of light – another new element – as a result of which he can walk upright as a human being. Later it proves that this spark of life is not present in all human beings, and that human beings are divided into two groups by this difference. I assume that Irenaeus's account of this element in Satornilus's teaching is too brief to do him justice. Anyway, Irenaeus gives the impression that the basis of receiving this spark is an immutable divine predetermination, but he does not mention whether or how it is possible for human beings to convert.

In this myth, Platonic terms are applied to the Redeemer: he is called 'unbegotten', 'incorporeal' and 'formless'. This means that he is eternal, imperishable and divine, and thus does not come from the created world but from the highest God. After being described in these terms, the Redeemer is identified as 'Christ', whose task was above all to destroy the God of the Jews. Here it emerges how Satornilus gave not only the Old Testament but also Christian faith a distinctive interpretation.

This emerges again in connection with his view that the Redeemer showed himself only seemingly as a human being, and thus had not really been a human being of flesh and blood. This docetic element, which is consistently Platonic, also occurred in the teaching of the Simonians.

Irenaeus reports of Satornilus's followers that they abstained from marriage and procreation, since these things were said to have been introduced by Satan. It emerges from this that according to Satornilus, marriage and procreation had not come from the creator angels but were introduced by Satan only after the creation. No other motive for this ascetic way of life, which also included vegetarianism, is given here.

Finally, it is striking in Irenaeus's account that there is no mention here of gnosis or a similar term, but only of trust in Christ as a condition for redemption. It appears from this that in this respect Satornilus remained close to the current Christian confession. Nevertheless he diverged from the catholic Christian view that the Father of Christ is the God of the Old Testament and thus the Creator of the world. Like Menander and the Simonians, Satornilus is a witness to a dualism between a highest God who sends a redeemer on the one side and the lower angels who are responsible for the creation of the world on the other.

2. The Secret Book of John

2.1. The tradition of the Secret Book of John

The Apocryphon or Secret Book of John must have been an important writing, since it has been handed down in various manuscripts. It occurs in books II, III and IV of the Nag Hammadi collection, in a shorter and a longer version. The fact that this Secret Book of John comes first in these three books (or *codices*) confirms the impression that this was regarded as a fundamental work. Moreover this work has been handed down in the Berlin Gnostic Codex, and Irenaeus offers an account which corresponds with part of it and which probably goes back to an earlier version.[5] It is also very important that the material of this Secret Book of John appears in a related form in a number of other works from Nag Hammadi. Their titles are: the Gospel of the Egyptians, in two versions (both times it comes after the Secret Book of John); the Hypostasis of the Archons; the Origin of the World (in two copies); the Three Steles of Seth; Melchizedek; Marsanes; Allogenes; and the Trimorphic First Thought. In addition, Irenaeus has also handed down similar myths, which, while diverging on all kinds of points, do show a clear affinity to it.[6]

Those who begin to read this Secret Book of John without any prior initiation will lose their way soon after the introduction in the many names of heavenly powers. So it has all the characteristics of an inaccessible and obscure work. This Apocryphon is rightly called an *apocryphal* book. But for those who want to learn about ancient gnosticism it is important to take note of them, however tough the pages which follow may be to read. Alien though this text is, all kinds of elements occur in it which will seem familiar after the discussion of Simon the Magician, Menander and Satornilus. Evidently at that time there was a need to supplement the already existing myths and thus to explain more accurately (or more fantastically) what had preceded the origin of this material world. Here we must keep in mind that ultimately fundamental questions of life are being discussed here. These include, for example: What does the highest God have to do with our world? What is our place in this body and in this world? How can we human beings learn to know the true God?

In order not to make matters more complicated than they already are, in principle I shall proceed from the shorter version which appears in the Berlin Codex and, in a slightly different form, in Nag Hammadi Codex III,1. This short version was presumably composed around 200. I shall refer to the longer version and the account given by Irenaeus only when they clarify the shorter version or seem to offer a better text. As is to be expected from a summary discussion, I shall pass over all kinds of details. I shall usually pay no attention to traces of insertions, from which we can infer what an older and even shorter version may have looked like. Similarly, I shall not discuss the many versions or clarifications in the other related works or accounts.[7]

In contrast to the previous discussions of the various myths, I shall not first describe the whole book and then make some comments on it. Because of the length and inaccessibility of this book I have divided the discussion into short sections, and I shall give some explanatory notes for each section immediately. In Part II I shall go more extensively into the background of this kind of myth.

2.2. The content of the Secret Book of John

2.2.1. The occasion for the vision (1–3)

For those familiar with the Gospels in the New Testament this book begins on familiar ground. John, the brother of James – here too they are called 'the sons of Zebedee'[8] – is addressed in the temple at Jerusalem by a Pharisee named Arimanias.[9] This Arimanias asks where John's master is, whereupon John says that his master has returned whence he came.[10] It seems from this that this encounter takes place after Jesus' crucifixion and resurrection. Arimanias says that this Nazorean – Jesus – was a deceiver who had led his disciples away from the ancestral traditions. This criticism saddens John; he goes to a lonely place on the mountain – perhaps the Mount of Olives is meant. There he asks himself about the Redeemer, the Father and the aeon to which we shall go from here (the Greek *aion* means eternity, but also 'heavenly sphere' or 'heavenly power'). John recalls as a saying of Jesus the words 'this aeon has assumed the form of the imperishable aeon', and he remembers that the Redeemer has not explained this.

2.2.2. *The divine appearance (4–5)*

At that moment heaven opens, a light shines and the whole world begins to quake. In the light a young man appears to John. He turns into an old man. He makes himself known as the Father, the Mother and the Son, and announces that he will communicate to John knowledge about the invisible and the visible and the perfect human being. John must then proclaim this knowledge to his spiritual kin of the 'unwavering race of the perfect Man'. (This refers to those who have true insight and participate in the redemption.)

2.2.3. *The Father (6–11)*

The revelation in which John shares is first about the Father, who is also called the holy Spirit and transcends all gods. He is utterly perfect, indescribable, indivisible, immeasurable, invisible, eternal, inexpressible, incomprehensible. To use a modern term, this Father is completely transcendent; he surpasses all notions that a human being can have of a god. Nevertheless he is described as the pure light, the eternal life, the blessed one, knowledge, the eternally good, mercy and grace; and it is said that he also distributes these properties.

2.2.4. *The Mother (12–18)*

As source of the Spirit, this Father made living water stream out and saw his own image in this water. The thought of this became independent and is called (among other things): perfect foreknowledge, likeness of the light, perfect power, First Thought. Her name was Barbelo.[11] She is the first human being, the virgin Spirit, and is at the same time male and female.

At her request the Father granted that some aeons should arise from her: Foreknowledge, Indestructibility and Eternal

Life. Thus together with the Thought and Barbelo herself, five aeons are enumerated.

2.2.5. *The Son (19–22)*

When Barbelo looked in excitement at the Father, she bore a spark of light. That is the Only-begotten, the Self-Procreated, the Firstborn Son of the All, namely of the Spirit of the Pure Light. The Father rejoiced over him and anointed him Christ with his goodness. (This is a play on words: for Greek ears 'Christos' had two meanings: 'anointed' but also 'good'; the latter was spelt *chrēstos* but pronounced *christos*.)[12]

At his request to the Father, the aeon Consciousness came into being. The Will, the Word and the Truth also arose. It is said of Christ that he has created everything by the Word and that he has received all power.[13] (But there is no mention here of the material creation of the world.)

2.2.6. *Four lights and twelve aeons (23)*

Four great lights arose from Christ and Indestructibility to stand by Christ, the Self-Procreated, and to be set over four aeons. In total, twelve aeons are grouped round these lights, most of which were not yet mentioned. Grace, Truth and Form belong to this first light, called Armozel. Foreknowledge, Perception and Memory belong to the second light, Oroiael. Understanding, Love and Idea belong to the third light, Daveithai (Irenaeus writes David). Perfection, Peace and Wisdom or Sophia belong to the fourth light, Eleleth.

2.2.7. *The heavenly Adam, Seth and his descendants (24–25)*

From Foreknowledge and the perfect Consciousness and with the approval of the great invisible Spirit and the Self-Procreated there arose the perfect, true human being, Adam. The Spirit set him over the first aeon, that of Armozel, and gave him an unconquerable spiritual power.[14] Adam praised the Spirit because all had come into being through him, and he praised the Self-Procreated, the aeons and the Father, the Mother and the Son.[15]

Adam set his son Seth over the second aeon, that of Oroiael. In the third aeon, that of Daveithai, are set Seth's seed or descendants, namely the souls of the saints. The fourth aeon, Eleleth, becomes the place for the souls which have not immediately been converted.

By way of explanation: certain gnostics regarded Seth as their prototype and forefather. This derivation is based on the Greek translation of Gen. 4.25, where Seth is called the 'other seed' that God brought into being. The redeemed who had attained the true knowledge saw themselves alluded to here. However, this origin from Adam and from Seth and his generation still takes place completely in the heavenly world of the aeons.

2.2.8. *The tragic fruit of Sophia's thought (26–28)*

According to this revelation, the aeon Sophia or Wisdom (23) played a tragic key role in this heavenly prehistory of the world. Without the approval of the Spirit, she herself thought a thought: she wanted to produce her own image from herself without a partner. This thought was called 'lascivious', 'lewd', and did not remain without fruit.[16] The result was ghastly: she brought forth an abortion which looked like both a lion and a snake. Sophia cast her fruit far from her so that the other aeons would have no knowledge of it, and set up a throne for it in the midst of a cloud of light. She called him Yaldabaoth, which possibly means Lord God of the powers; however, this name is also explained as child of chaos.[17]

This description of the throne in a cloud of light points to the Old Testament, which speaks of the throne of God and of the fiery pillar of cloud in which the Lord is present.[18] It is also in accord with the Old Testament that Yaldabaoth partly looked like a lion.[19] So Yaldabaoth means the God of the Old Testament.

2.2.9. *Yaldabaoth creates his own aeons and angels (29–37)*

Yaldabaoth, the 'first ruler' (in Greek *archon*, the singular of *archontes*) filched a power from his mother and created an aeon of blazing fire. He united himself with his ignorance[20] and brought forth twelve lower angelic powers after the model of the imperishable aeons, each of which was given its place in its own aeon. Seven angels in turn came to stand under each of them; in total 360 angels were created. This division is apparently based on an astrological system. Various angels' names recall Hebrew names for God: thus some of the twelve are called Yaoth, Adonaios, Sabaoth and Adonin.[21]

Some Hebrew divine names can also be recognized in the names of the seven angels or archons who rule over the seven heavenly spheres. Six of them are given an animal face: Yaoth is like a lion, Eloaios like an ass, Astaphaios like a hyena, Yao like a snake with seven heads, Adonaios like a dragon, Adoni like an ape, and Sabbataios has a face of blazing fire.[22] Yaldabaoth associated seven powers with each of these seven angels, namely – in the same order – Foreknowledge, Divinity, Lordship, Envy, Kingship, Understanding and Wisdom. Yaldabaoth himself, also called Saklas ('foolish'),[23] gave the angelic powers a share in his own fire and power, but not in the power which he had withdrawn from his mother Sophia. So he was their lord and he could be called God by them.

2.2.10. *Yaldabaoth's arrogance and Sophia's repentance (38–41)*

The Creator Yaldabaoth looked at his creation and the many angels and said, 'I am a jealous God, outside me there is no one'.[24] As a commentary on this, it is said that with this acknowledgment that he is jealous, he already indicated that there is another God. Of whom would he be jealous otherwise?

When Sophia saw the consequences of her autonomous deed, she began to wander around. This is connected with Gen. 1.2, where it is said that the Spirit (according to the Greek translation, the Septuagint) was driven over the waters: this is related to Sophia, who went to and fro in the darkness of ignorance. She was ashamed of herself and showed penitence. Her brother aeons then made intercession for her, whereupon the invisible Spirit – the Father – granted that she should return to the fullness (the *pleroma*) of the aeons. She was brought back and lodged in the ninth aeon, until she had made good her failing; this ninth aeon was two aeons above the creation of Yaldabaoth.[25]

2.2.11. *The creation of Adam's soul body (42–45, 51–54)*

Then a voice resounded which said: 'the Man exists and the Son of Man'. This was a correction of Yaldabaoth's arrogant exclamation that there was no one but him.[26] Yaldabaoth heard this voice and thought that it had come from his mother Sophia. Then the Father showed his 'likeness' in human form. The seven archons saw the form of this image in the water and said, 'Let us make a human being after the image of God and after the likeness' (cf. Gen. 1.26). Their seven powers (see 2.2.9) made a human being with a 'soul' body, whom they called Adam. (This body of soul substance was thus immaterial.) However, these seven powers were not capable of raising this man up; nor could the 360 angels do this.

However, Sophia wanted to receive back the power which Yaldabaoth had taken from her and asked the Father for this. He sent the Self-Procreated – Christ – with the four lights to Yaldabaoth; they advised him to blow some of the spirit that was in him into Adam's face. When Yaldabaoth blew this power of Sophia into Adam's soul body, it began to move (cf. Gen. 2.7). With the help of this stratagem, Sophia's power – also called 'spirit' (*pneuma*) – came into Adam. The seven angels then became jealous, because they comprehended that Adam was more understanding than they. Therefore they placed him in the lowest region of matter, on the earth.

Then the Father had pity on the power of Sophia which was in Adam and sent his good Spirit as a helper, also called the 'Understanding of the Light' and 'Life'. (Here we can already recognize the figure of Eve, who in Gen. 2.18, 20 is referred to as Adam's helper and whose name according to Gen. 3.20 means 'life'. Her creation is only described later, in 61–62.)

2.2.12. *The creation of Adam's material body (55)*

Because the human being, Adam, shone from the light that was in him and his thought surpassed that of his creators, the angels made a body of earth, water, fire and wind. These four elements are interpreted as symbols of matter, darkness, desire and the hostile spirit. This material body was put on Adam and (in accordance with Platonic philosophy)[27] is regarded as a bond to matter and as a tomb for every human being.

2.2.13. *Paradise and the two trees (56–59)*

Yaldabaoth put Adam in paradise, which he misleadingly called a pleasure for him; in fact this paradise with its so-called 'tree of life' (Gen. 2.9) led to godlessness and death. By contrast, the 'tree of the knowledge of good and evil' (Gen. 2.9) is called the 'Understanding of the Light'. Granted, Adam received the command not to eat of this tree of the knowledge of good and evil, but Christ triumphantly tells John that he – and therefore not the serpent – had persuaded them[28] to eat of it nevertheless. He says that the serpent taught Adam procreation through desire, pollution and corruption.[29]

2.2.14. *The creation of the woman (60–63)*

Because Adam was more understanding than Yaldabaoth, Yaldabaoth, jealous as he was, wanted to take back from Adam the power which he had given him. Therefore he put him in a stupor by veiling his senses. The power, now identified with the 'Understanding of the Light' (the name given both to the tree in 58 and Adam's helper Life in 54), stayed hidden in him, but Yaldabaoth wanted to produce her out of his rib. Although he did not get hold of this Light, he then created a woman with part of the power hidden in Adam.[30] This course of events is expressly distinguished from Gen. 2.21–22, where 'Moses' says that the woman is formed from the man's rib.

When Adam came to his senses and the Understanding of the Light took the veil from his mind, it was like waking out of drunkenness and a shock of recognition. He recognized in the woman bone of his bone and flesh of his flesh. Then comes the quotation that for this reason a man will leave his father and mother and cling to his wife, and that the two shall be one flesh (Gen. 2.23–24). Adam called her the Mother of all living beings (Gen. 3.20).

Adam now learned from Understanding, which appeared as an eagle, to eat of the tree of knowledge and to recall his perfection. According to the longer version Christ reveals that he himself – in accord with 58 – appeared in the form of an eagle to both of them and taught them to eat of the tree of knowledge.

It thus seems that Yaldabaoth's plan to rob Adam of his inner power and Understanding of the Light has failed and that, on the contrary, after discovering his other half, Adam has arrived at a deeper insight.

2.2.15. *Curse and procreation, Cain and Abel (64–65)*

When Yaldabaoth understood that Adam and the woman had distanced themselves from him, he cursed them. He stipulated that the man should rule over the woman, cast them from paradise and clothed them in gloomy darkness (cf. Gen. 3.16–24). But they did not dare to curse him and make his ignorance known to the other angels.

Then Yaldabaoth fathered two sons by the woman: Yaue with the face of a bear and Eloim with the face of a cat.[31] Eloim was righteous and was set over fire and wind; Yaue was unrighteous and set over water and earth. With other names they are also called Cain and Abel (cf. Gen. 4.1–2); they are set over matter and over material bodies. Yaldabaoth also placed the desire for procreation in Adam. Thus sexual desire arose through his doing.

2.2.16. *The procreation of Seth (66)*

Adam then fathered Seth (cf. Gen. 4.21). The Mother (Barbelo) then sent her Spirit to the woman so that this Spirit remained active in Seth's seed or generation. In these descendants the redeemed recognized themselves (cf.25).

2.2.17. *Eternal redemption (67–69)*

Prompted by this mention of Seth, the prototype of the redeemed with true knowledge, John asks whether all souls will be redeemed. Christ says that the answer to this will only be given to the 'unwavering race' (cf. 5; this is the generation of Seth). All human beings have 'the power' (namely, their soul) in them. Moreover those on whom the Spirit of Life descends will be redeemed and rise to the great lights. They have fought against the evil impulses in their fleshly body and have overcome these, so that they will inherit eternal life. By contrast, others get a counterfeit spirit in them which puts them on a false trail. Nevertheless their soul, or the power that is in them, can overcome the counterfeit spirit and escape the evil deeds. Thanks to the 'imperishable care', they will still be redeemed and receive the rest of the aeons.

2.2.18. *The fate of the souls without knowledge (70–72)*

When John asks about the fate of the souls who have acquired no knowledge, Christ says that the counterfeit spirit has made these souls heavy, has appointed them to evil deeds and has cast them into forgetfulness. After life in the body, such a soul comes into the hands of Yaldabaoth's angelic powers. These put her in fetters and make her wander round in their course above the earth until she attains knowledge and so is redeemed.

She can still acquire this knowledge from a soul which does have the Spirit of Life in it. When such a soul rises and goes along the angelic powers, a soul held fast there which does not have knowledge can gain insight and travel above with her. That a soul which lacks knowledge must first of all be reincarnated is emphatically ruled out.

2.2.19. The fate of the lapsed (72)

However, there is one exception to this prospect of complete redemption for all souls with and without true insight. When souls have learned to know this true insight but have then lapsed from it, eternal punishment awaits them. Torment and punishment is thus the fate of anyone who has blasphemed the holy Spirit.[32]

2.2.20. The influence of the counterfeit spirit to the present day (73–76)

John has one last question: where the counterfeit spirit comes from. Christ's answer contains a continued exposition of the first chapters of the book of Genesis. He explains that the generation of the perfect Adam, i.e. those who had a part in the seed of the Mother – also called the holy Spirit and the Understanding of the Light – were wiser than Yaldabaoth. When Yaldabaoth saw this, he took counsel with his angelic powers and they produced the fate which from then was to rule over all gods, angels, demons and human beings.

Then Yaldabaoth repented of all that he had done and resolved to send a flood over all that human beings had done (cf. Gen. 6.5 etc.). The Mother, Foreknowledge, had warned Noah about this. But when he proclaimed what would happen, people did not believe him. Only the people of the unwavering race (the generation of Seth) hid themselves in a shining cloud and thus not, as Moses said, in an ark. Meanwhile darkness spread over the earth. (From this it appears that there was no inundation of water but of darkness.)

Then the angels of Yaldabaoth went to the daughters of men to procreate descendants from them for their pleasure (cf. Gen. 6.1–4). But they did not succeed the first time. They created the counterfeit spirit, changed themselves outwardly into the consorts of the women and thus fathered children of the darkness with them. They also brought gold, silver, copper, iron and gifts for the people. The consequence was that the people no longer thought of Foreknowledge, and through the action of the counterfeit spirit hardened their hearts. This situation holds 'to the present day'.

2.2.21. *Conclusion (77–79)*

The first and last words of a closing hymn are cited; only in the longer version is this included in full. It appears to be about the threefold descent of Foreknowledge to earth to make known the true redemption there.

Finally Christ says to John that he must write these things down and hand them on to the unwavering race in secret. He curses anyone who hands them on for a gift or for food or drink or clothing. After that he disappeared, and John began to tell his fellow-disciples what had been told him by the Redeemer.

2.3. *Retrospect on the Secret Book of John*

To conclude with, here are a few remarks on this Secret Book of John.

First, it can be seen that this revelation is a very free interpretation of the first chapters of the biblical book of Genesis. The first four chapters of Genesis deal with the creation of heaven and earth, with Adam and Eve, paradise and the reasons why they are driven out of it, and with Cain, Abel and Seth. In the Secret Book of John we find a revision of this against the grain. Genesis 6, which is about angels who take to themselves wives on earth and about the flood, also undergoes a similarly wayward interpretation at the end of the Apocryphon.

Secondly, this revelation here and there takes up the Gospels which are known from the New Testament.

Thirdly, the many heavenly powers which are mentioned are dominated by the threefold revelation of the Father, the Mother and the Son, as John receives this in the beginning. That this highest divine power is threefold suggests the confession in catholic Christianity that God reveals himself as Father, Son and holy Spirit. However, apart from this agreement it is striking that in the Apocryphon this threefold nature is given divergent content. The God of the Old Testament, here called Yaldabaoth, is emphatically not the same as the highest Father who revealed himself in the beginning to John.

In respect of the prototype of the human being, Adam, it becomes clear – and this is the fourth point – that he is composite. His body and soul are the product of the seven lower powers of creation, who correspond to the seven planets. (In addition, there can be a connection with the Jewish notion of seven archangels.) By contrast, his spirit comes from Sophia, who belonged to the highest aeons around Christ. It also appears that humankind is subdivided into different groups. Those who partake of the true knowledge and are redeemed by it go back to Seth. Others allow themselves to be led by the counterfeit spirit, but they can get away from it.

Fifthly, this Apocryphon remains unclear about the figure of the Redeemer. We read how Christ makes known the revelation of the true knowledge to John. But at the end it is said of the Mother, who is also called Barbelo and Foreknowledge, that she descended three times to earth to make known the true redemption.

3. Passwords for the return of the soul

3.1. The journey along the planets

According to Satornilus and the Secret Book of John, seven powers or archons had created the human being and ruled his life on earth. These seven powers return in numerous versions of these gnostic myths. They are always to be located in the spheres of the seven planets which were distinguished at that time, namely the moon, Mercury, Venus, the sun, Mars, Jupiter and Saturn.

According to a Platonic notion, after death the human soul had to arise from the body along the planets to the stars.[33] Anyone who regarded the archons in the heavenly spheres at the height of the seven planets as being inferior or jealous had every reason to dread this future journey of the soul. So 'pass-words' were taught which made it possible to pass by these archons unhindered. If the soul spoke the correct password at each planet, the angelic powers were compelled to let it pass through on its way above.

These passwords do not occur in the myths discussed so far. However, as I have remarked, there are numerous variations on these texts, some of which contain the necessary words. For example, such a password can be found in the first Revelation of James and, in a related form, in Irenaeus. The Second Book of Jeu contains as many as fourteen passwords.[34]

3.2 *The First Revelation of James*

According to the first Revelation of James, some days after his apparent suffering,[35] Jesus made known to his brother James how he could pass the powers in the heavenly spheres. On his way above he would be watched out for by 'toll collectors' or frontier guards who would want to take not only toll but also his soul. Jesus prepared his brother – and thus anyone who had a part in the knowledge of redemption – for the following dialogue. One of the toll-collectors would ask:

> 'Who are you or where are you from?'
> You are to say to him, 'I am a son, and I am from the Father.' He will say to you, 'What sort of son are you, and to what father do you belong?'
> You are to say to him, 'I am from the Pre-existent Father, and a son in the Pre-existent One. I have come to behold all things, both those which belong to myself and others' . . . 'To the place from which I have come, there I shall return.' And if you say these things, you will escape their attacks.[36]

The answer to the question 'To what father do you belong?' is of great importance. The soul must have knowledge of the most High Father who transcends all things and existed before all the others (and thus is 'pre-existent'). If the soul of the dead person only knows of the lower archons, like the

God of the Old Testament, then it will not get through their sphere of power, and their frontier guards can have power over it.

3.3 *Mark the Gnostic*

Irenaeus does not describe the above dialogue, but he does give the essential password for the archons. However, in his work the context is rather different from that in the Revelation of James. He describes how the followers of Mark the Gnostic were accustomed to anoint a dying person with oil mixed with water, and to utter conjurations over him. When the initiate died and thus left his body on earth, he had to say to the archons the password that he had learned during his earthly life. After these words they would have to flee.[37]

3.4 *The Ophites*

A number of passwords which in a sense connect up with the Secret Book of John have been handed down by Origen and are attributed by him to the Ophites, or, as he calls them, Ophians. This name is derived from the Greek *ophis*, which means 'snake', and refers to the snake in paradise who led Adam and Eve to eat of the forbidden fruit (Gen. 3). Now Origen does not mention the whole myth of the Ophites, but Irenaeus has handed it down – in brief.[38] Their myth seems to have all kinds of features in common with the Secret Book of John, while sometimes diverging from it quite markedly. Thus the origin and rise of the aeons is described differently. Certainly Yaldabaoth occurs in it, with six powers which have emerged from him; their names – which are now familiar to us – are Yao, Sabaoth, Adonaios, Eloaios, Horaios and Astaphaios.[39] One difference from the Secret Book of John is that paradise with the two trees is not situated on earth but in the higher immaterial world of the aeons. There, according to the Ophites, the snake led Adam and Eve to eat of the tree of the knowledge of good and evil and thus to attain the true knowledge. So this differs from the Secret Book of John, where Christ claims this role for himself (see 2.2.13).

The Ophites thought that because of this transgression of the commandment Yaldabaoth had at that time cast them from heaven into material bodies on earth.

The information which Origen gives about the Ophites is to be found in his detailed defence of Christian faith called *Against Celsus*.[40] In it the names of the seven archons are Yaldabaoth, Ya or Yao, Sabaoth, Adonaios, Astaphaios, Aiolaios or Eloaios and Horaios.[41] Origen gives the passwords necessary to get by these archons – only Adonaios is left out.[42]

For example, to pass through the sphere of Yaldabaoth on the farthest planet Saturn, the Ophites learned to say (not, it seems, without flattery):

And thou, Yaldabaoth, first and seventh, born to have power with boldness, being ruling Word of a pure mind, a perfect work for Son and Father, I bear a symbol marked with a picture of life, and, having opened to the world the gate which thou dost close for thine eternity, I pass by thy power free again. May grace be with me, Father, let it be with me.

Origen also gives the password for the power which is said to rule in the eighth sphere, i.e. outside the sphere of the seven archons. In Origen's text this power has no name, but possibly the Ophites were referring to the Leviathan, the snake which in their view surrounded the whole world with its seven planets and their spheres.[43] To pass him the soul had to say:

Solitary King, bond of blindness, unconscious oblivion, I hail thee, the supreme Power, preserved by the spirit of providence and wisdom (Sophia). From thee I am sent in purity, being already part of the light of Son and Father. May grace be with me; yea, Father, let it be with me.[44]

This kind of password formed the final portion of the knowledge which human beings could acquire to leave earthly life behind them and return to their origin with the most high God. Thus one could learn from the beginning to the end how human beings had come to this earthly life and how after death they could again be redeemed from this existence in the material body. But there is also evidence of the other possibility, namely that the souls who had not acquired the correct knowledge to pass the powers would be thrown back on earth. Their lot was to be reincarnated in another body.[45]

Part II   Backgrounds to gnosticism

5

The origin and purpose of life

At some points in the previous chapters I remarked that the myths discussed there gave answers to the great questions about the origin and purpose of life on earth. These questions about life are not in themselves 'gnostic', but at that time were asked in very different milieus. The questions show not only deviations but also remarkable agreements. Here, first, are four examples of them from non-gnostic circles. After that I shall discuss two texts in which these questions are put in a 'gnostic' perspective.

1. *Lucius Annaeus Seneca*

Lucius Annaeus Seneca lived in the first century of our era. In Rome he had instruction in rhetoric and philosophy. He travelled to Egypt, where he got to know Eastern customs and religions. He was entrusted with the education of Nero, who was later to become emperor; he also advised Nero when Nero came to power. However, this relationship was destroyed in his old age. At that time he wrote a number of letters to his friend Lucilius on ethical and philosophical questions.[1] In one of these letters he gives a brief survey of the different starting points of the philosophies of Plato, Aristotle and the Stoics. He writes as if Lucilius does not think the questions he is discussing are important and then asks him:

> May I not ask what are the beginnings of all things, who moulded the universe, who took the confused and conglomerate mass of sluggish matter, and separated it into its

parts? May I not inquire who is the Master-Builder of this universe, how the mighty bulk was brought under the control of law and order, who gathered together the scattered atoms, who separated the disordered elements and assigned an outward form to elements that lay in one vast shapelessness? Or whence came all the expanse of light? And whether is it fire, or something even brighter than fire?

Am I not to ask these questions? Must I be ignorant of the heights whence I have descended? Whether I am to see this world but once, or to be born many times? What is my destination afterwards? What abode awaits my soul on its release from the laws of slavery among men?[2]

In another letter Seneca shows that in connection with these questions he attached great importance to finding the right *knowledge* of himself and of nature:

Therefore, gird yourself about with philosophy, an impregnable wall. Though it be assaulted by many engines, Fortune can find no passage into it . . . Let us then recoil from her [Fortune] as far as we are able. This will be possible for us only through knowledge (*cognitio*) of self and of the world of nature. The soul should know whither it is going and whence it came, what is good for it and what is evil, what it seeks and what it avoids, and what is that reason which distinguishes between the desirable and the undesirable, and thereby tames the madness of our desires and calms the violence of our fears.[3]

So we can see how Seneca, as an old man looking back on his life, resorted to philosophy in his search for answers to the great questions of life. A year or two later (in 65) he was accused of plotting against the emperor Nero and was advised to put an end to his life. He followed this advice: he regarded death as the end of the imprisonment of his soul in the earthly body.

2. Clement of Rome

The second example is briefer. It, too, comes from Rome, from the Christian church there. Around 96 this church wrote a letter to the church in Corinth, where there was great unrest. According to the oldest tradition the author of this letter was called Clement, and he was 'bishop' of the church in Rome. After an appeal for solidarity between the strong and the weak and the rich and the poor in the community, he makes this comment about the origin and birth of the human being.

> Let us consider, then, brethren, of what matter we were formed, who we are, and with what nature we came into the world, and how he who formed and created us brought us into his world from the darkness of a grave, and prepared his benefits for us before we were born.[4]

Clement's view of things is that human beings have received all goodness from God the Creator, so that 'we ought in everything to give him thanks'.[5] He then describes his own comments on the Christian faith with the words 'we have looked into the depths of the divine *knowledge* (*gnosis*)'.[6] With his appeal to this knowledge, Clement aimed at driving away the unrest and disunity from the Christian community in Corinth.

3. Akabya ben Mahalalel

A third example of posing the great questions of life appears under the name of the Jewish teacher Akabya, the son of Mahalalel. He lived in the first century of our era in Israel. In one of the writings of the Mishnah[7] we can read how he expressed these questions and how he answered them.

> Keep in view three things and thou wilt not come into the power of sin. *Know* whence thou comest and whither thou goest and before whom thou art to give strict account.

Whence thou comest, – from a fetid drop. Whither thou goest, – to the place of dust, worms and maggots: and before whom thou art to give strict account, – Before the king of the kings of kings, the Holy One, blessed be He.[8]

Thus Akabya strongly emphasized the lowly descent and inconspicuous destiny of human beings. He thought that if people were aware of this it would keep them from sin. With a view to this he also emphasized that people need to lead their earthly life in such a way that they can be responsible before God. Here Akabya was certainly thinking of a life faithful to the law of Moses and the traditions based on it. That he introduced the great questions by saying '*Know . . .*' (*da'*) indicates the importance that he attached to correct knowledge in avoiding sin and doing good.

Akabya's summary of the key points of life found acceptance. This text recurs at various places in ancient Jewish literature, sometimes in an expanded form.[9]

4. *Philo of Alexandria*

The following example also comes from a Jew, named Philo, who lived in Alexandria in the first half of the first century. Unlike Akabya, whose words have been handed down in Hebrew, Philo spoke and wrote Greek. In a long series of lengthy commentaries on the 'five books of Moses' he drew richly on Greek philosophy. Thus he wanted to show the degree to which these books of Moses corresponded to Greek philosophy. In his commentary on Gen. 3.24–4.1, Philo explains that God gave his creation on loan and that nothing in itself is perfect, so that the one needs the other. Thus human beings have themselves on loan. They are composed of a soul and a body and seem to have mind, reason and sense without these really belonging to them.[10] Philo then formulates the following questions.

Where was my body before birth, and whither will it go

when [I have][11] departed? . . . Whence came the soul,
whither will it go, how long will it be our mate and com-
rade? Can we tell its essential nature? When did we get it?
Before birth? But then there was no 'ourselves'. What of it
after death? But then we who are here joined to the body,
creatures of composition and quality, shall be no more, but
shall go forward to our rebirth,[12] to be with the unbodied,
without composition and without quality.[13]

In respect of correct *knowledge* Philo goes on to say that in
this life we do not so much know ourselves but we are known.
He explains this by saying that the soul knows us without it
being known by us.[14] In these views Philo seems to identify
human beings during their earthly lives strongly with their
bodies. The soul, which according to him is added to this,
seems to have its own knowledge of the human being. At the
same time the soul guarantees the continuity of human existence after death, when human beings live on no longer as a
'composite' but without a body.

5. Theodotus, pupil of Valentinus

The great questions which occupied people came to light, in
different variants, in the four previous examples. We also
know a Christian-gnostic variant of them, which Clement of
Alexandria noted in his excerpts from the work of Theodotus.
This Theodotus was a pupil of Valentinus; his work can be
dated around 160–170. The following quotation comes from
Theodotus' discussion of fate, which according to him is
determined by the powers that govern the course of the stars
and planets. (We should think of these powers, among other
things, as the angelic powers or 'archons' which appeared in
the previous chapter.[15]) The powers of fate also decided on the
moment of each person's birth. According to Theodotus,
Christ, the Redeemer has destroyed the influence of fate and
of these powers. This means that whoever is baptized in the
name of the Father, the Son and the holy Spirit need fear

nothing more from fate and the astrologers.[16] But it is not only baptism which brings redemption from this but also gnosis, i.e. the answer to the following questions:

> Who were we? What have we become? Where were we? Whither have we been thrown? Whither are we hastening? From what have we been redeemed? What is birth, what is rebirth?[17]

Beyond doubt these were the subjects which Theodotus discussed in his baptismal catechesis. It is evident how here he went into the human anxiety about the fate that rules over everything, to which Seneca also alluded. Thus although this kind of question was not specifically gnostic but universally human, the answers into which Theodotus initiated his disciples were based on a quite distinctive *gnosis*. Christian gnostics like Theodotus derived this 'knowledge' on the one hand from the Old Testament and from the writings which were later called the 'New Testament'. On the other hand, the gnostic interpretation of these was largely inspired by the philosophy of the time. Before we discuss the biblical and philosophical sources of gnosticism, here first of all is a critical voice which takes up the matters we have been discussing.

6. Tertullian's verdict

In one of his polemics against the heresies which threatened the catholic church, Tertullian (c.200) goes into the origin of these other tendencies. Here he refers to the 'worldly wisdom' of philosophy and then mentions the Greek philosophers Heraclitus, Plato, Aristotle, Epicurus and the Stoics with their founder Zeno. He thinks – with some justice – that the questions which the 'heretics' posed were posed by philosophy.[18] In his words:

> The same subject-matter is discussed over and over again by the heretics and the philosophers; the same arguments

are involved. Whence comes evil? Why is it permitted? What is the origin of man? And in what way does he come? Besides the question which Valentinus has very lately proposed – Whence comes God?[19]

The questions, which in the preceding examples are not yet put so pointedly, are striking: 'Whence comes evil? Why is it permitted?' 'Whence comes God?' It seems from all this that Tertullian did not want anything to do with these audacious questions or with a Christianity tinged with philosophy. However, the development of early Christianity in its many manifestations ('catholic' and 'gnostic' in all kinds of variants) shows that these questions were unavoidable. In the following chapters we shall discuss some answers which were available in the world of the time.

6

The Jewish religion

In fact all religions and philosophies go into the questions where human beings come from and what their task and destiny are in this world. This is also true of the religion of the people of Israel. The previous chapter contained two Jewish texts from the first century of our era. Now we shall go back to the books of Israel's 'instruction (*torah*, also translated law), prophets and writings' which Christians usually call the 'Old Testament'. The majority of these books were written in Hebrew and translated into Greek from the third century BCE onwards. According to an ancient tradition the translation of the five 'books of Moses' (the *torah*) was made in Alexandria by seventy or seventy-two Jews. So this translation is called the Septuagint (also LXX), which means 'seventy'. The other Old Testament books were also translated into Greek later and added to the Septuagint. Moreover the Septuagint contains a number of books and additions which are not in the Hebrew Bible; they are now called 'deutero-canonical'.

Through this Greek translation the books of the Jewish religion became accessible to the Hellenistic world, of which the Jews formed a part. Because the views of a number of 'gnostic' teachers and writings are also based on the Septuagint, I shall regularly refer to this Greek translation.

A number of the Old Testament narratives have been handed down in a more extensive form in other Jewish books which are not included in the Old Testament. The value of these traditions is that they bear witness to beliefs from the time before and around the beginning of our era. So they form part of the background to gnosticism. Therefore I shall also pay attention to these elaborations of the Old Testament.

1. The first chapters of Genesis

1.1. The creation of the world and the first human beings

In Greek, the first book of the Bible is called Genesis,[1] which means 'coming into being', 'origin' and also 'birth'. It begins with two different creation myths. The first chapter relates how in the beginning God created the heaven and the earth in six days. The Hebrew for God is *elohim*. Really this is a plural and thus means 'gods', but everything suggests that here one God is meant. *Elohim* is also translated as a singular in the Septuagint: *ho theos*, literally 'the god'.

On the sixth day, when the plants and the animals had already been created, God said: 'Let us make the human being (*adam*) in our own image, as our likeness'. The task of the human being was to rule over the animals and over the earth and to populate the earth. God created the human being 'male and female'. At the end of this first creation story it is said that all that God had made was very good (Gen. 1.1–2.3).

In the second creation story the Creator is not called just *elohim* in the Hebrew, but *yahweh elohim*. In the Greek translation, *yahweh elohim* is sometimes rendered 'God' (or really 'the god'), but sometimes, in full, 'the Lord God' (*kyrios ho theos*). It had become customary among the Jews not to speak the name *yahweh* and to read *adonai* instead, which literally means 'my lords'.

According to this account, the human being (*adam*) was the first creature that the Lord God made on earth: he formed him from dust of the ground (*adama*) and blew into his nostrils the breath of life. After that the Lord God planted a splendid garden (*paradeisos* in Greek) in Eden full of fruit trees, including a 'tree of life' and a 'tree of the knowledge of good and evil'. The human being might eat of all the trees in the garden, but eating from the tree of the knowledge of good and evil was forbidden him on pain of death (Gen. 2.4–17).

After the Lord God had created the animals, he finally formed a woman from the human being's rib. The snake was able to persuade the woman that if she and her husband were to eat of the tree of the knowledge of good and evil they would be 'like God' and would know good and evil. In the Septuagint 'like God' is translated as 'like gods' (in agreement with the Hebrew plural). When they had eaten of the forbidden fruit they became afraid of the Lord God. As a consequence of their transgression the Lord God cursed the snake and the earth. He also decreed that the woman would bear children with pain and that the man would have to toil in order to be able to eat from the earth. Their lives would be finite, and after their death they would return to the dust of the earth from which they had been formed. They were driven out of the garden; angels barred the entrance (Gen. 2.18–3.24).

The Hebrew term for the man, *adam*, has become a proper name in Gen. 2 and 3. His wife is called 'the living one'; in Hebrew this is *chawwa*, which in Greek becomes *eua*. Adam and Eve had two sons, whom they named Cain and Abel. Because the Lord (his name is now simply Yahweh) accepted a sacrifice from Abel but not one from Cain, Cain became angry. Cain was warned about his anger by the Lord, but he nevertheless killed his brother. Cain was cursed by the Lord for this. Cain then went away from the Lord (Gen. 4.1–16).

This – in broad outline – is the mythical account of the creation of the world and the experiences of the first human beings according to the book of Genesis.

1.2. *Notes on the first chapters of Genesis*

In the following interpretation of this mythical beginning of the world we are concerned with the later Jewish and gnostic use of it. So I shall pass over the original context in which these stories were written. My approach to these primal stories begins from the 'big questions' which arose in Chapter

5, and falls into two parts. First I shall go through the text in as unprejudiced a way as possible. After this first benevolent and to some degree uncritical reading I shall, secondly, put some critical questions to the text, of the kind that was raised by people in the Hellenistic world, including the 'gnostics'.

1.2.1 Uncritical approach

First of all a comment about the twofold creation narrative: the way in which the compiler of Genesis has combined these two versions gives the impression that he regarded them as supplementing each other and in no sense as contradictory.

According to Genesis, the answer to the question 'Where do we human beings come from?' is that human beings are created body and soul by God, also called the Lord God. This God is imagined as the Creator of heaven and earth, who has made all things very good. Originally he created human beings as man and woman and put them in a paradise.

This raises the question why humankind today is far from living in a paradise. If God made everything so good, where does all the suffering and pain come from? The answer to this is indirect and narrative. Suddenly, there in the garden was the snake, who made an sneaky proposal to the woman. Because the woman and the man were then disobedient to the command of the Lord God, the Lord God pronounced a curse on the earth and on human beings. From then on their lives would be marked by pain, troubles, hard labour and death. All the suffering and misery in the world thus arise from human disobedience and God's punishment for it. Cain's murder of Abel typifies the violence that has afflicted humankind since then.

The answer given to the question why human beings are on earth is that the woman must bear children and the man must rule over her and must sweat it out on the accursed earth in order to provide for his livelihood.

Finally, where do we human beings go after death? We return to the dust of the earth from which we were formed.

Therefore the human being is called *adam*, which is associated with *adama*, 'earth'.

1.2.2 *Critical approach*

However, a critical approach to these stories of the beginning leads to other questions. Where does this creator God come from? Why does he have different names? Why are we not told about the creation of the angels? Where does the matter come from with which he gave form to creation? To whom did he say 'let us make the human being . . .'? Why is the creation of the world and human beings reported twice? Doesn't the commandment of the Lord not to eat of the tree of the knowledge of good and evil show that this God is petty and narrow-minded? Who is the snake, and how does he come to know that those who eat of this tree will be like God (or gods)? Isn't the curse on the earth and human beings pronounced by the Lord God more a proof of his own inability? Doesn't the fact that the Lord refuses Cain's sacrifice bear witness to his capriciousness? Why is nothing said about the ongoing existence of the soul, or the spirit, after death?

These are some critical questions which the first chapters of the book of Genesis could raise for readers from Hellenistic antiquity. It will immediately strike modern readers that some of these questions are still regularly asked.

2. *The curse on the earth and human destiny*

After the first chapters of Genesis, the 'fall' of Adam and Eve does not appear again as an explicit theme in the Hebrew Old Testament.[2] Certainly the prophets several times assert that the Lord strikes the earth with his anger and his curse,[3] but that is not the tone of the Old Testament as a whole. Here we also find more positive testimonies about the creation and the position of human beings in it. In Psalm 104, which is a song of praise to the Lord and his creation, sinners and evildoers are mentioned at the end, but the tone is set by God's majesty and the wisdom with which he keeps his creation in being. Sin and curse are not recalled here. The Leviathan, a mythical sea monster, is regarded as a plaything of the Lord. In Psalm 8 it is said that the Lord made human beings a little lower than a god (or gods).[4]

In the deutero-canonical book of the Wisdom of Ben Sirach the curse on earthly life is recalled with a certain degree of resignation. Jesus Sirach says of laborious work on the land that this is 'created' by the Most High.[5] In the deutero-canonical Wisdom of Solomon it is stated polemically that God did not make death and that the underworld does not rule over the earth. The author confesses that God has created all things to exist and remain in existence, and that no noxious herb forms part of this.[6]

However, other voices can also be heard. Questions are regularly asked about God's just governance and about the meaning of life and human suffering on earth. Thus the book of Job is a powerful protest against the suffering that comes upon Job undeservedly. In the book of Ecclesiastes it is emphasized firmly that human life is full of difficulty and seems meaningless. The author of this book initially asserts that everything – including human beings – has come from dust and will return to dust.[7] His expectations for an ongoing existence of human beings after earthly life then seem minimal.[8] But he ends his pessimistic observations with the statement that when a human being dies, the matter returns to the earth, but 'the spirit returns to God who gave it'.[9] Thus it seems that according to Ecclesiastes everything need not be over at a person's death.

This belief that God would receive the pious person after death gradually became more widespread among the Jews.[10] That God would not let human life be lost is also evident from the growing belief that the righteous will rise from the dead. Thus in the Septuagint there is an addition to the book of Job: 'It is written that he (Job) will rise together with all those whom the Lord shall raise.'[11] However, this resurrection can also be interpreted as an ongoing existence of the soul in heaven.[12]

The questions about the meaning of human life and the suffering in it could thus be answered in Israel with a reference to the resurrection of the righteous. Life in the resurrection or life with God would balance out the difficult life that many people led on earth.

3. God and the heavenly powers

3.1. The one God, the angels and the devil

Although different names are used for God in the Old Testament, nowhere is it said that he consists of several gods. Certainly, in Israel, initially different gods and goddesses were worshipped, but the confession 'Hear, Israel, the Lord is our God, the Lord is one'[13] resounds against this. Along these lines it is said in the book of Isaiah in the name of the Creator: 'I am the Lord, there is none other; beside me there is no God.'[14] This implies that according to the prophet, the worship of other gods and their images is empty.[15] Over against this, the existence of 'sons of God' in the sense of angelic powers is recognized.[16] A very common name for God is even Lord of the powers (*Yahweh tsebaot*). Evil spirits are also reckoned among these powers.[17] Finally, some passages speak of the *satan* ('opposer', 'accuser') as an evil power who is also reckoned among the sons of God.[18] In the Septuagint, in these passages *satan* is translated *diabolos* ('blasphemer'), from which our word devil is derived.

This devil is also mentioned in the Wisdom of Solomon, where in 2.23–24 it is said of the creation of the human being:

> But God created man imperishable, and made him the image of his own eternal self; it was the devil's spite that brought death into the world, and the experience of it is reserved for those who take his side.

However, it is not explained here, any more than in the earlier books of the Old Testament, where the devil and evil in the world originally come from. There are, though, more developed ideas about good and evil angels and spirits, as is evident above all from later books.[19] Where the book of Genesis relates soberly that the 'sons of God' had alliances with women on the earth, in the Book of Enoch dozens of names of these fallen angels and their seductive qualities are listed.[20]

The following tradition about the fall of the Satan and his angels also belongs in this angelology. When Adam was created in God's image, the angel Michael summoned the other angels to worship this image of God. However, Satan and the angels who were under him refused to do this, because they had been created earlier than Adam and thus Adam was lower in rank than they were. Satan threatened to erect his throne above the stars and to be equal to the Most High (cf. Isa. 14.13). Then the Lord God became angry and cast Satan and his angels down to earth.[21]

Thus this myth gives a partial answer to the questions which the Old Testament leaves unanswered, namely: how did Satan come to earth, and where does evil come from?

3.2. *God, Wisdom and the Word*

One development in later parts of the Old Testament is that the wisdom of God comes almost to be imagined as a separate person.[22] In the introduction to the book of Proverbs wisdom (in Hebrew *hokhmah*) is introduced speaking as a woman who calls for awe before the Lord. She bears witness that the Lord had 'acquired' or, according to the Septuagint, 'created'[23] her in the beginning, even before the creation of heaven and earth. This personification of wisdom (in Greek *sophia*) is continued and developed above all in some books of the Septuagint which do not appear in the Hebrew Bible.[24] In the Wisdom of Solomon this *sophia* is called 'the pure emanation of the glory of the Almighty', 'a reflection of the eternal light', 'a spotless mirror of the working of God and an image of his goodness'.[25] She is mentioned in the same breath as the 'holy Spirit'.[26] It is attested of her that she protected the 'first-formed' Adam when he alone was created, and that she has freed him from his transgression. She has also given him power to rule over all.[27]

This Wisdom is never identified with God. She remains a creature, but she is the first and highest creature who sits beside God on his throne.[28] Akin to this notion of Wisdom is that of the Word (*logos*) of God, also according to the book of the Wisdom of Solomon. Here we can read how in the silence of the night God's all-powerful Word sprang from the royal thrones in heaven into the doomed land as a powerful fighter. This land is meant to be Egypt, from which Israel is to be freed, but 'the doomed land' can also be translated as 'the doomed earth'.[29]

3.3. God as man and the son of man

Another tradition which comes to light in the prophet Ezekiel shows a human notion of God. In the sixth century BCE Ezekiel had a vision of the Lord God in Babylon. He speaks of something that seems like a throne on which he saw the likeness of the appearance of a human being (*adam*).[30] He seems to be struggling for words when he tries to describe God. The appearance of God seems to him to be most like that of a human being. This corresponds to Gen. 1.26, where it is said that God wanted to create the human being in his own image and likeness.

In the second century BCE another Ezekiel, surnamed the Tragedian, described Israel's exodus from Egypt in the form of a Greek play. In it Moses relates that he had a dream on Mount Sinai of a throne which reached to the corners of heaven. On it sat a noble man with a crown on his head and a staff in his hand. He gave the staff to Moses and invited him to go and sit on the throne.[31] With a different accent, the Greek word for 'man' used here (*phōs*) also means 'light', and can therefore possibly be translated 'light-man'. This human figure indicates a manifestation of God in his glory.

A human characterization of God is also given in the book of Daniel, which likewise dates from the second century BCE. He is described as an 'Ancient of Days' on a flaming throne. According to this vision, however, 'someone like a son of man' receives the royal rule over all peoples from this Ancient of Days.[32] So the book of Daniel gives a glimpse of the notion that a human figure reigns alongside God in heaven. This 'son of man' alongside God also appears in the apocryphal book of Enoch, which was written about the same time.[33]

In the later rabbinic literature (from the second century CE and later) various different pieces of evidence are to be found about a second power alongside God in heaven. The story about Elisha ben Abuyah from the beginning of the second century is striking: in a vision he ascended to the heavenly paradise. He thought that he could see the angel Metatron sitting on the throne there. After that he held the view that there were 'two powers'.[34] However, this vision, which was also shared by others, was rejected as heretical in the rabbinic literature.[35]

3.4. *God's unity and the powers alongside God*

Thus it seems from the previous sections that the Jewish religion knew good and bad angels, properties of God which were almost imagined as personal, and a son of man alongside God. Usually these notions were not thought to conflict with the unity and sovereignty of the Lord God. Thus the power of the devil remained subordinate to the power of God. The personifications *sophia* and *logos* came from heaven but could only appear and free people in the name of God – and thus not independently. The heavenly son of man also received his royal rule from God. From these notions emerged the view that there were 'two powers' in heaven, though this was rejected as heretical. These are important observations for the rise of gnosticism (and that is equally true of the rise of Christianity).

4. *'Knowledge' in Judaism*

The previous discussions were about the place of human beings in the creation and about the one God, who, however, according to Judaism seems to have been able to have other powers alongside him. Yet another theme from Judaism deserves attention in conclusion: that of true 'knowledge'.

Chapter 5 contained some examples from which it proved that people from very different backgrounds sought the correct *knowledge* about life and about God. The Old Testament, too, is about the true knowledge. In the Septuagint, the word *gnosis* is one of the terms used for this. This term appears above all in books about wisdom. Thus according to the Septuagint Prov. 2.6 says that 'the Lord gives wisdom, from his face come *gnosis* and understanding'; and in 16.8: 'whoever seeks the Lord will find *gnosis* with righteousness'. Wisdom of Solomon 2.13 and 14.22 are about the godless who wrongly think that they have '*gnosis* of God'. By contrast, God's wisdom gives 'the *gnosis* of the holy' (10.10). These examples from the Septuagint could be multiplied tenfold.[36] This 'knowledge' is usually knowledge of the Lord God who reveals himself to the pious person.[37]

In the Hebrew the term *da'at* is often used for this knowledge. Once in the Old Testament this word refers to insight into God's plans for the end time.[38] However, the term *da'at* occurs regularly not only in the Hebrew Old Testament but also in other Hebrew texts. Thus it is said in the Qumran writings that the children of truth received 'the spirit of knowledge' and that they hold 'the truth of the mysteries of knowledge'.[39] The Eighteen Benedictions, which in their earliest form come from the first century CE, contain the prayer: 'Grace us for your sake with knowledge (*de'ah*), insight and understanding. Blessed are you, Lord, you grace us with knowledge (*da'at*).'

This knowledge which Jews sought and for which they prayed was directed to Israel's God, the Lord, and usually related to the knowledge of his instruction and the doing of his will. But it could also be secret knowledge of God's plans for the world. Thus in all kinds of ways the Jews looked for answers to the questions what life in this world was for and where God would lead humankind.

7

Plato, Philo and Platonic philosophy

The name of Plato (430–347 BCE) has already been mentioned several times. This Greek philosopher is extremely important for understanding later gnosticism. In his youth in Athens, Plato had come under the influence of Socrates. Later he wrote a number of dialogues which centre on this Socrates. In these conversations Socrates indefatigably put critical questions to others who thought that they had certain knowledge, about the knowledge they supposed they had.[1] Although he himself had a good deal to say, he did not aim at developing a philosophy with firm outlines. In his view, the true philosophy implied that a person continued to seek wisdom all his life. For him therefore 'astonishment' was *the* principle of philosophy.[2]

In the footsteps of Socrates, Plato too was restrained in setting down a complete philosophical doctrine in writing.[3] For this reason he made his readers witnesses to these dialogues; by thinking through them they could make the possible conclusions their own. Sometimes Plato had one of the conversation-partners relate a myth; this did not need to be believed literally, but it was very evocative.

However, it was inevitable that later philosophers would try to make a systematic whole of Plato's dialogues and the myths that were related in them. Here I shall be concerned above all with this later use, and not primarily with Plato's original intentions. In my discussion of Plato and his influence on later authors, like the Jew Philo, I shall limit myself to some themes which recur in gnosticism.

1. *Plato's dialogues*

1.1. *The doctrine of ideas and the purpose of life*

In a dialogue which is called *Phaedo,* after one of those engaged in it, Plato describes the last conversation of Socrates before his death. Socrates had been condemned to drink a cup of poison, because people thought that he was dissuading the youth from traditional religion.[4]

In this dialogue Socrates says that at death the soul detaches itself from the body. Only then will the soul, apart from the body, be able to learn reality truly; for the body prevents the soul from having any part in truth and knowledge. According to Plato, Socrates began from the higher reality of the 'forms' (often translated as 'ideas') of, for example, justice, beauty, goodness, greatness, health, power and so on. As long as the soul is tied to the body, in visible reality we can learn the effects of these 'forms', but our knowledge of them is and remains defective. The body is in fact a source of misery; it can become sick and produces desires and anxiety, war and violence. Anyone who wants to live a virtuous life must therefore be prepared for death. The goal of earthly life is for the soul already to purify itself during this life and to learn to live in accordance with the most important virtues; these are sobriety, justice, bravery and insight. After life in the body the soul can then learn to know these virtues in their pure 'forms' or 'ideas'. It will then, says Socrates according to Plato, be able to live in the company of the gods. For the soul belongs to the divine, and the body to the mortal.[5] In another dialogue Socrates states the purpose of life thus: that one becomes as like to God as possible by living justly, piously and with insight.[6]

1.2. *To attain knowledge is to remember knowledge*

Plato taught that human souls were immortal. This means not only that a soul lives on *after* the death of the body, but also that it already existed *before* life in the present body. So a soul can have belonged to another body; Plato taught the transmigration of souls or reincarnation.[7] It is more important in this context that according to various of Plato's dialogues the soul originally comes from the high heavenly world of 'forms' or 'ideas'. When the soul still dwelt there, it came to know this highest reality in heaven. On being born into a body, the soul lost this knowledge, but during earthly life it is possible to regain this knowledge by bringing it into oneself. Thus the acquisition of knowledge in fact consists of a person learning to recall the original knowledge of heavenly reality. It also becomes clear from this what the purpose of life on earth is: to be guided by this higher reality that transcends our material world by recalling this higher world.[8]

1.3. *The origin of the world according to the* Timaeus

At the end of his life Plato wrote a dialogue in which a certain Timaeus expounded the origin (*genesis*) of the world and of humankind. This Timaeus is not interrupted as he does so; thus it is presupposed that Socrates and some others listened to his monologue with approval (*Timaeus* 27a, 29d).

Timaeus recognizes that the Maker and Father of the universe is difficult to discover. He indicates that one can speak about the origin of the universe only in terms of probability. But Timaeus does begin from the existence of a Creator. For 'Creator' he uses the term *demiourgos* (rendered in English as demiurge); this really means artisan, but also denotes a person in authority. Timaeus imagines that this Creator has made the world from disordered matter on the basis of a model (*paradeigma*). The Creator was good and indeed wanted to make a good and attractive world which would be as like him as possible in goodness (28c–30a).

How did he go to work? From the prevailing disorder he made an ordered, round world of fire, earth, water and air; roundness was regarded as the most perfect form. The world received a soul and mind from the Creator and thus is a living being. Timaeus calls the world a god, although it does not exist from the very beginning. The Creator is also god, but with the difference that he already *is* from the beginning (30a–34b).

The Creator ordered heaven in accordance with the model and produced seven planets, including the sun and moon. They are imagined as living beings with souls. He also created the stars: according to Timaeus they are 'the heavenly generation of the gods'. Timaeus is reticent about the lower gods (*daimones*) of mythology, but he does mention Earth and Heaven, Oceanus and Tethys, Phorcys, Cronus and Rhea, Zeus and Hera. He recognizes that they descend from the (higher) gods (37c–41a).

The gods (both the stars and the mythological gods) received from the Creator the task of making three sorts of living beings, which hitherto had existed only as 'forms'. These three sorts of living beings are the birds, the water creatures and the land animals, but Timaeus first discusses only the creation of human beings. The Creator declared that if he were to make these living beings himself they would be like gods, whereas it was his purpose that they should be mortal. The Creator did first prepare a large number of immortal souls; he gave one of these to each star. He made known to these souls the laws determined by fate. If they were transplanted into bodies, they had to guide their conflicting feelings into good paths and live a righteous life. Then after the death of the body they would return to the star in heaven whence they had come. Should, however, a soul fail in a male body, it would have to be born again and turn into a woman. If there was still no improvement, then the human being could turn into an animal in a following life. The Creator made these ordinances known to them because he who alone was good did not want to incur any blame for what they would do later. After that he sowed the souls over the earth and over the planets and withdrew (41a–42e).

The 'young gods' then imitated their Creator, made bodies of fire, earth, water and air, and put the immortal souls in their heads. But their creatures were not at all perfect; the human being is depicted as one who is often mistaken in his perceptions and has become deceitful and uncomprehending. Although his soul comes from the heavenly world and has received all kinds of knowledge there, it is without understanding when it is attached to a mortal body. Through growth and feeding and a good upbringing, however, the human being can become completely sound and healthy (42e–44e).

Timaeus thinks that the gods also placed a mortal soul in the human breast, which knows passions like pleasure and pain, daring and fear, malice and hope. Moreover under the midriff of the human being the gods attached a third kind of soul which, like a wild animal, is greedy for food and drink (69c–70d). According to him, the origin of the birds and the animals on land and in the water are to be explained as reincarnations of human beings who had lived badly in a former life and sunk ever deeper (91d–92c). By contrast, the purpose of human life on earth is for human beings to go by the order of the universe and thus reach the very good life that the gods have prepared for them (90d).

1.4. The supreme divine principle

The *Timaeus* repeatedly speaks of the Creator of the world, but in earlier dialogues Plato called the divine principle that orders and rules everything 'Mind' (*nous*).[9] Anyone in search of this supreme Mind as the creating and ordering principle in the *Timaeus* can possibly read it into the work,[10] but Plato does not emphatically denote the Creator as Mind there.

Plato uses yet other terms for the supreme divine principle in other dialogues. This does not mean that all these designations have precisely the same meaning. I shall pay special attention to one term. In the dialogue called the *Republic*, Socrates discusses the education that the rulers in the ideal republic must receive. The question is: how do they partake in the highest knowledge which is necessary for a good government? Socrates then introduces 'the idea of the Good'. In 1.1 I already mentioned the idea of goodness along with other 'ideas' or 'forms' which can be found in higher reality. In the

Republic it now seems that Socrates here attributes the highest status of all to the idea of goodness or the Good. He says that the idea of the Good is the highest knowledge, and also the cause of knowledge and truth. Of all the knowledge that a human being can gain, the idea of the Good is the last and most difficult to know. But, Socrates says, according to Plato, once someone has seen the Good his soul longs for the higher world of what really *is*. Socrates calls 'the Good' the most shining part of 'the Existent'. According to him, anyone who has attained this insight must be in a position to rule a republic wisely and justly.[11]

There is no mistaking the fact that here the idea of 'the Good' has taken on the features of the supreme divine principle. In other dialogues, however, this highest place is assigned to 'the Beautiful' and 'the One'.[12] We can see from this difference in ideas that in his dialogues Plato did not present a complete philosophical system.

1.5. Notes on Plato's dialogues

From this selective account of some elements from these dialogues, we can see how Plato occupied himself with the question of the purpose of human life on earth. Closely connected with this is the question how human beings came on earth. Plato began from an invisible higher world of 'forms' or 'ideas' which were worked out in the visible lower world. The 'model' from which the Creator created the visible world corresponds to these 'ideas'. Plato also calls this Creator 'Mind'.

However, he does not make it clear whether the ideas are as old and eternal as the Creator, or whether for example they come from the Creator and thus are his thoughts. At the end of this chapter (4) it will prove that this lack of clarity over the origin of this model of the ideas had important consequences.[13]

From the distribution of tasks which the Creator made before the creation of the human being it proves that the human being is a 'composition'. Human beings have an immortal soul which comes from the Creator and which is sown from the starry heavens. However, the 'young gods' made the human body from the perishable elements of fire, earth, water and air. Moreover this body has a mortal soul full of wavering passions and in addition a third, lustful soul.

According to Plato, the purpose of human beings on earth is that they should remember the high origin of their soul and learn to live virtuously in accordance with this. Those who live virtuous lives on earth will learn to know the original 'forms' or 'ideas' of the virtues in heaven after the death of the body. There they will lead a blissful life in the company of the gods. So the purpose of human beings lies in this return on high. By contrast, the soul which does not gain the correct knowledge of the higher world of the virtues is doomed to return to earthly life. So it must be reincarnated.

Here we have the expression of a strikingly dualistic view of human beings, i.e. a division between the immortal soul and the perishable body.

In our consideration of the idea of 'the Good' in Plato's *Republic* it proved that there this 'Good' has the features of the supreme divine principle. Now the *Timaeus* speaks of the Creator, and there he is called 'god' and 'good'. It also states that God is responsible only for the good and not for evil.[14] But this supreme idea of 'the Good' which we find in the *Republic* does not recur in the *Timaeus*. For the moment I shall simply note the cardinal question which these two dialogues have raised, namely: what is the relationship between 'the good' in Plato's *Republic* and the Creator in his *Timaeus*?

2. Philo's exposition of the books of Moses

2.1. Philo of Alexandria and Greek philosophy

All kinds of elements from the dialogues of Plato recur in the Jew Philo of Alexandria. In Chapter 5 I already remarked that in his commentaries on the 'books of Moses' he drew richly on Greek philosophy. The starting point for his commentaries was not the Hebrew Bible but the Greek translation of the Septuagint.

Now of course Greek philosophy after Plato was not a single whole. Philosophers after him, like Aristotle and the Stoics, had tried to resolve obscurities in Plato's works or had quite different views. In the centuries around the beginning of our era it had been customary to integrate the various philosophical currents as far as possible. Thus gradually different mixed forms of Hellenistic philosophy arose. The philosophy which to an important degree remained orientated on Plato is called 'Middle Platonism'.

The influence of Plato is dominant in Philo, but he is equally influenced by the interpretations of Aristotle and by the philosophy of the Stoics. However, in discussing Philo, I shall not go into the specific origin of those ideas which do not originally occur in Plato.

As in my comments of Plato, I shall discuss only some subjects which are important for understanding later gnosticism out of the many which Philo has to offer.

2.2. The Creation of the World

Philo's work *The Creation of the World*, which is about the first three chapters of the biblical book of Genesis, would be incomprehensible to anyone who was not familiar with Plato's *Timaeus*. However, in antiquity the *Timaeus* had become a well-known work. Since this creation myth of Plato's had several points of contact with the biblical creation story, it was obvious to Philo that he should refer to both.[15]

Philo explains that the creation in six days according to Genesis 1 is not about the material creation but about the invisible model (*paradeigma*) that God conceived. Indeed he speaks of the 'forms' or 'ideas'. He also took over Plato's term for Creator, namely demiurge (*demiourgos*) (16–22; 36).

Philo also calls the invisible world of God's model the 'Word (*logos*) of God'. Philo thinks that he can read about this 'Word of God', this conceived model of the visible world, in Gen. 1.27, which speaks of the 'image of God'. Thus in his view this image is the whole of the invisible world of the 'ideas' (24–25; 31).

According to Gen. 1.26, God said, 'Let us make human beings in our image and likeness'. From Philo's commentary I shall distil four observations on this.

First, this is not about the visible earthly man, but only about his imperishable mind (*nous*), i.e. the guiding part of his soul. God has no body, and so there can be no question of the creation of the human being in both mind and body. According to Philo the human mind can in a sense be called 'god' (69).

Secondly, the human mind is created in the image of God. The image of God is the model, or 'Word of God', and not God himself. Thus this model stands between the human being and God. Indeed the human mind is the imitation of the model (or the image of the image) and thus only indirectly an image of God himself (25).

Thirdly, when God says in the plural 'Let *us* make human beings', according to Philo this means that God had 'fellow-workers'. Philo had observed earlier that God needed no one to give him advice (23), but he has a suggestion why God did not act alone in the creation of human beings. Unlike the other creatures the human being has a 'mixed nature'; this means that he is open to both good *and* evil. But according to Philo (and according to Plato) God alone is good, and he cannot at the same time be the cause of anything bad. Therefore because human beings would also be able to do evil, God handed part of his creation over to his 'fellow-workers'. Thus God was the cause of the good in human beings, namely their imperishable spirit, and these fellow-workers would be responsible for the evil in human beings. So God himself would remain free from evil. However, it is left vague precisely who these fellow-workers are (72–75).

Finally, it should be noted that according to Gen. 1.27 this human being is 'male and female'. According to Philo this means that this human being, in incorporeal form, is undivided (76).

According to Philo, the description of the creation of the invisible model of the 'ideas' is concluded in Gen. 2.4–5 (129–130). The next description (in Gen. 2.7) is of the creation of the visible man, body and soul. God modelled him from the dust of the earth, and after that he breathed the breath of life into his face. This man is 'composed' of the dust of the earth and of an immortal soul. Philo also calls this soul 'a divine breath' or 'Spirit' (*pneuma*) (134–135).

Here Philo does not speak of 'fellow-workers' who have to help God with the creation of the human being. He is highly idealistic about this first human being of flesh and blood. He calls him truly good and fair, a temple for the reasonable soul, far more excellent than the humankind which degenerated afterwards; this human being lives in accordance with the divine law of nature (136–143).

However, things went wrong with this human being when the woman was made. Then the original unity was broken and mutual desire and sexuality and procreation arose. At this time, according to Philo, injustice and transgressions of the law began (151–152).

Philo's view is that the purpose of human beings is for their mind (*nous*) to acquire knowledge of the higher world and rise to God, the great King. Along this way the mortal human being will become immortal (70–71; 77).

2.3. *Notes on* The Creation of the World

Much more could be quoted from Philo's commentary on the first chapters of Genesis. Thus I have left out of account his expositions of paradise, the serpent as the symbol of desire and the expulsion from paradise (153–169). Here it is important that Philo has taken over Plato's idea of a double creation. On the one hand there is the model with the 'ideas', and on the other there is the concrete visible result. The influence of Plato is also evident when Philo explains that the Creator used 'fellow-workers' for the creation of the human being. But there is an important difference. In Plato the young gods are charged with the making of the visible human body, whereas Philo mentions the 'fellow-workers' in connection with the invisible creation of the human mind. When it comes to the modelling of the human being in body and soul, then according to Philo God does this himself.

Plato and Philo agree that God alone is *good* and cannot be the cause of evil. But there is also a difference here. In Plato the Creator takes account from the beginning that the souls will make wrong choices later in their earthly bodies; in order not to bear the blame for this, he warns them about this from the start. The young gods are not made responsible for this later evil. In Philo, by contrast, the later evil in human beings is attributed to the contribution of God's 'fellow-workers'.

These views in Philo's book *The Creation of the World* do not stand in isolation. Similar explanations also occur, sometimes in a somewhat different or strongly divergent form, in his other works.[16] There God's fellow-workers are identified as his 'powers' (*dunameis*), which are said to stand above the angels.[17] He also says of these powers that they were involved in the creation of the whole world, because it was inappropriate for God himself to touch disorderly matter.[18] If we keep to *The Creation of the World*, it appears that here Philo can give a striking answer to the question why the creation is described twice in the book of Genesis.[19] He connected this twofold account with Plato's *Timaeus* in a way that can be called ingenious, or possibly artificial. But he also regularly keeps a distance from Plato. This is evident for example when according to Philo God himself finally models the visible human being.

2.4. *Plurality in the one God*

A number of points which are to be understood from their philosophical background also appear in Philo's other works. As in his work *The Creation of the World*, the Platonic influence here is powerfully present.

Sometimes Philo indicates that God is plural. He is quite certain that God is one and pours scorn on pagan polytheism.[20] But as already emerged earlier, Philo also speaks of 'powers'. He can speak of 'a power by which the universe was made, one that has as its source true goodness'.[21] He attests that a voice in his soul says that although God is truly one, his highest powers are two in number: namely his goodness with which he created everything and his power with which he governs everything. He states that these two powers are held together by a third power, his Word (*logos*).[22] Philo also names 'God' and 'Lord' as the two highest powers of 'the Existent'; this term for the one most high God comes from Exod. 3.14 in the Septuagint.[23] As one power of 'the Existent', 'God' (*theos*) is said to stand for his creative power and goodness and grace; as the other power of 'the Existent', the 'Lord' is said to stand for his ruling and punitive power.[24] Philo once says that no one can really swear by God, since God is unknowable, but we can swear by God's Name, i.e. by the Word (*logos*) that interprets God. He calls this Logos 'God of us, imperfect', and goes on to speak of 'the First' as God of the wise and perfect.[25]

Another plurality in God appears when Philo speaks of the procreation of the world. God, the Creator and Father, had intercourse with his own knowledge (*episteme*), which Philo here calls 'Mother'. Thus God fathered (literally 'sowed') a creature in her, and after her birth-pangs she bore God's only beloved son who is visible, namely this world. For this Philo quotes the biblical book of Proverbs, 8.22, where Wisdom (*sophia*) says: 'God acquired me as the first of his works, and before eternity he established me.' Philo understands this text to mean that God's knowledge and Wisdom is the Mother of the whole creation.[26]

Philo was clearly convinced that these distinctions in God were not in conflict with God's unity. But a great tension in his thinking emerges here. It is easy to see how later thinkers – like the gnostics – worked out these distinctions further without maintaining God's unity so firmly.

2.5. *The origin and destiny of souls*

According to Plato, the souls of humankind come from the stars; during life on earth they are temporarily attached to a material body or incarnated. In the footsteps of Plato, Philo also speaks about this descent and incarnation of the souls. For him, the fact that the soul comes from heaven means that it is its destiny to return to heaven. In the body, the soul is in fact a stranger who longs for the heavenly fatherland.[27] At one point Philo says that some souls which had already risen again could return here out of longing for the earthly life; thus he seems in passing to agree with the possibility of reincarnation.[28]

In these texts about the heavenly origin of the soul Philo does not write that in heaven she gained the knowledge that she can later recall on earth. But elsewhere he refers affirmatively to the Platonic view that learning is based on recollection.[29] He also writes about the sparks of knowledge (*epistēmē*) which God has sown in us.[30]

This theme of the 'knowledge' of God occurs countless times in Philo's works. He usually speaks of *epistēmē*, but he also uses the word *gnosis*. Thus he writes that wisdom leads to the final goal, the knowledge (*gnosis* and *epistēmē*) of God.[31]

2.6. *Retrospect on Philo of Alexandria*

In this chapter on Plato and Platonic philosophy, Philo has been discussed as a witness to the influence of Plato's philosophy from the first century of our era. However, deep down Philo is no Middle Platonic philosopher, but a Jew who is widely influenced by the Greek philosophy of his time. The distinctive thing about Philo is that he tried to express the Jewish religion in terms which had become current in the Hellenistic world. In other words, Philo is on the one hand a witness to later Platonism, but on the other – and no less – he is a witness to the 'Hellenizing' of Judaism. Moreover it will appear (in Chapter 9) that in Philo all kinds of views occur which are worked out further in gnosticism.

3. Two Middle Platonic philosophers

As a Jew, Philo of Alexandria felt tied to the confession that God is one. Although in this respect we can put critical questions to his views which indicate a plurality in God, God's unity was and remained for him the starting point of his Hellenistic expression of the Judaism.

That was not the case with Hellenistic philosophers who had no ties to Judaism. I shall now sketch some developments which are in line with Platonic philosophy, in the person of two philosophers from the second century of our era. These developments shed particular light on gnosticism from the same period.

3.1. Alcinous's introduction to the teaching of Plato

Around the year 150, one Alcinous wrote a handbook on the teaching of Plato. In it he offers some answers to questions which Plato had left unanswered, namely about the relationship between 'the Good', the ideas and the Creator. Of course Alcinous, too, leaves some things unexplained, but the direction in which he is thinking is clear.

Alcinous is concerned with the knowledge of what truly *is*, i.e. of the first causes and basic principles of the world. He uses both *epistēmē* and *gnosis* for 'knowledge'.[32] He begins from the existence of the 'first God'. He also calls this first God 'the Father', 'Cause of all', 'the first Mind' (*nous*), 'the Good', and 'the God above heaven'. According to Alcinous the 'forms' or 'ideas' are the thoughts of this most high God. These ideas together form the eternal 'model' for the world (9–10; 27; 29).

This most high, eternal and essentially unnameable God is the Origin and Father of the Mind of heaven and of the soul of the world. Alcinous also calls this Mind of heaven the Creator (demiurge). This Creator is likewise God, but of a lower status than the most high God (7; 10).

The most high God leaves the working out of his 'ideas' or his 'model' to this Creator. On the basis of this the Creator formed the world out of matter: the earth, the seven planets and the stars. In his turn the Creator handed the creation of the animals and human beings over to his children, the (lower) gods. Because the Father, the first God, had provided immortal souls for the human beings, the Creator sent these souls down from the stars. In order not to bear any blame for the evil into which they could fall in human bodies, the Creator explained the laws of fate to the souls before he let them descend. As Lawgiver he warned them of the passions that they must avoid and taught them about justice. Anyone who lived an unrighteous life would have to be reincarnated in a woman in a second life and after that in an animal (12; 14–16; 25).

According to Alcinous, the purpose of life on earth is for human beings in their minds to be as like as possible to God in heaven by living virtuously. He explains that this God in heaven is the Creator, and not the God above heaven, because the latter transcends virtue. The soul which on earth has recalled the knowledge of the higher world and has observed this will return after her life in the body to the star in heaven whence she came. There she will be in the company of the gods. According to Alcinous, both the souls of the gods and those of human beings have a 'gnostic capacity for discernment' (25; 28–29).

From Alcinous's description of the cosmos we can make out that the way up which the soul has to take lies through the seven planets and along 'the eighth power that encompasses all things'. This eighth power is not identified more closely. Then the soul arrives at the stars, which in accordance with Plato Alcinous presents as gods (14–15).

3.2. *Numenius of Apamea*

That Alcinous was not alone in his interpretation of Plato is clear from, among others, Numenius of Apamea in Syria. He wrote some books in which he referred to Pythagoras and even to Moses, both of whom he regarded as Plato's teachers.

These books have been lost in their entirety, but all kinds of fragments of them have been preserved in quotations in later writers.[33]

In a similar way to Alcinous, Numenius speaks of the 'first God', whom he also calls 'the Good', 'the One', 'the Existent', 'the first Mind' (*nous*) and 'King'. Secondly, according to Numenius there is the 'second God', namely the Creator (demiurge) of the world, whom, like Alcinous, he also calls 'Mind' (*nous*) and 'Lawgiver'. This second God, the Creator, is good, because he partakes in 'the Good', the first God . The first God is in fact also called 'Father of the creator God'. Thirdly, Numenius sometimes speaks of the third God, by which he means the world. But elsewhere he explains that the second and third God are one; from this it seems that he regards the Creator as the divine principle of his creation, the world. The Creator made this world by establishing himself on the 'forms' or 'ideas' of the first God (frs 11–21). Numenius interprets Pythagoras and Plato as saying that God is the beginning and cause of the Good, whereas matter is the beginning and cause of evil. According to Numenius, the world, which is composed of the goodness of the 'form' (or 'idea') and the badness of matter, therefore stands between good and evil.[34]

On mankind, Numenius thinks that the first God sowed all souls as seed, while the Creator saw to it that they found their way 'into us' (fr.13). He describes how the souls descended to earth from the Milky Way through the constellations and the planets (frs 31–32; 34). On earth the souls which are destined to it can partake of the divine Mind (*nous*) that has been sent down to them (fr.12). They then attain to the beautiful knowledge by recalling their heavenly origin (fr.14). Numenius thinks that those who want to deal personally with 'the Good', the first God, must detach themselves from all that is perceptible by means of a 'divine method' (fr.2).

Just as the souls have descended to earth, so after death they can rise again from the body to the Milky Way. But in order to be admitted to this way on high, they must first be judged by judges in the centre of the earth: for this Numenius refers to Plato. However, he interprets him to say that this 'centre of earth' is somewhere in heaven. The judges who have their seat there have the authority to allow the souls to rise to the starry heaven or not to let them go further than the planets.[35] Numenius certainly expected that this last category of souls, which does not get higher than the spheres of the planets, has to be reincarnated. However, this theme is only mentioned in passing in the fragments of his that have come down to us.[36]

4. *Retrospect on Plato and Middle Platonism*

Alcinous and Numenius give an indication of some interesting developments in Platonic philosophy which also appeared in Philo, though in Philo they sometimes remained more concealed. In Chapter 9 I shall work out in more detail how these developments shed a clear light on different central aspects of the gnosticism of this same period.

The most striking thing about Alcinous and Numenius is their view of the highest God and of the Creator. It proved that Plato spoke on the one hand of the Good, the Beautiful and the One, and on the other of the good Creator and Father. However, Plato left his readers uncertain about the mutual relationship between these designations of the highest divine being, although a particular interpretation was available. This interpretation comes to light without disguise in Alcinous and Numenius. They begin from a 'first God', who is essentially unnameable, but whom they denote with various Platonic terms like the Good, the God above heaven, the Father, the first Mind, Cause of all, the One. This first God conceived the forms or ideas for the model of the world. But the first God does not have anything to do with the matter which was already present. The first God hands over the forming of the formless matter in accordance with his ideas to the Creator, whose Father he is. Designations of this Creator or demiurge are: Mind, the second God, Lawgiver. This Creator creates order in the formless matter by building on the forms or ideas of his Father, the first God. This gives a clear answer to the question which was put in 1.5 of this chapter in connection with Plato. In fact the Middle Platonic philosophers aim to give an interpretation of the sentence in the *Timaeus* that the Maker and Father· of this universe is difficult to find. People read into it a distinction between the Maker (or the Creator) and the Father (or the first God). Now anyone who re-reads 2.4 about the plurality of the one God in Philo in the light of this distinction will see that Philo too must have been familiar with this view. He is certainly influenced by it, but as a Jew he did not want to drop the fundamental confession of the unity of God.

Given the distinction between a first and second God, it is interesting to see what task is assigned to which God. Thus it appears that the immortal souls which are intended for human beings come from the first God, while the second God, the Creator, sees to it that they descend from the stars to the earth. Both Alcinous and Numenius call the Creator Lawgiver in this connection, since (in accord with the *Timaeus*) he must first make the souls acquainted with the laws of fate.

The striking thing about Numenius is that he sometimes calls the world the third God, while he regards matter as the beginning and the cause of evil. However, his designation of the world as the third God points above all to the divine Mind of the world, namely the Creator. For Numenius' negative evaluation of matter we should also think of Plato's view that the human body is a source of misery.

8

The mystery religions and early Christianity

The dissemination of foreign religions in the Hellenistic world is one of the phenomena which give us an insight into the rise of gnosticism. In the fourth century before our era, Alexander the Great had conquered numerous peoples in the Middle East and united them in one great empire. Since then an intensive exchange and fusion of cultures and religions had come about, and this continued even after this great empire had fallen apart. Later the Romans, from the second century before the beginning of our era, had subjected many of these peoples to their authority. In this Roman empire, too, adherents of Persian, Babylonian, Egyptian, Jewish, Syrian, Greek and Roman religions and religions from Asia Minor had come to know one another's gods and myths. Here it was natural to look for similarities between the gods of the different peoples and to compare corresponding gods. Nevertheless, people did sometimes opt for the special worship of another god. This need not mean that they forswore the traditional gods of their forefathers. But it can certainly be inferred that the traditional religion no longer satisfied them in every respect. Some new religions are known as 'mystery religions' because people could be initiated into them with a secret ritual. Moreover, Greece had previously also already known such mystery religions on its own soil.

As an example I shall discuss the worship of Isis and Osiris. The dissemination of this religion in the first centuries of our era is to be seen as a parallel to the rise at that time of groups which are called 'gnostic'.

Another religion which arose at that time is Christianity. At that time Christianity, too, in some respects took on the features of a mystery religion. But the discussion of Christianity has another function than a random identification of a second example of a new religion which arose then. Earliest Christianity provoked all kinds of interpretations which are called 'gnostic' and thus form the theme of this book. On the one hand Christianity is to be regarded as a parallel to this gnosticism, but on the other it formed one of its breeding grounds.

1. *The worship of Isis and Osiris*

1.1. *Plutarch of Chaeronea on Isis and Osiris*

The worship of the Egyptian divine couple Isis and Osiris had already been introduced into Greece some centuries before our era. Their myth is described by Plutarch of Chaeonea.[1] He lived from around 46 to 120 and was chosen to be a priest of Apollo in Delphi around 95. At the same time, like Alcinous and Numenius, he was a Middle Platonic philosopher.

In broad outline the myth amounts to this. Isis and Osiris were brother and sister and loved each other: they had a son, Horus. Osiris ruled over Egypt and brought the Egyptians civilization and respect for the gods. However, his wicked brother Typho managed to shut him in a chest and dump it in the sea. Isis, in deep sorrow, began to look for this chest and found it. Thereupon Typho cheated her of the dead body of Osiris, divided it into fourteen pieces, and scattered these over Egypt. Isis found them again apart from Osiris's sexual organ, which had been devoured by a pike. From then on Osiris ruled over the underworld.[2]

Plutarch gives every possible mythological and philosophical explanation of this myth; I shall only mention the Platonic interpretation, which he himself prefers. He explains Isis as the feminine principle of creation. She was receptive to all 'forms' and 'ideas' and through her alliance with Osiris brought forth her son Horus, who is a symbol of this world.[3] Plutarch identifies Osiris with the Greek god Hades or Pluto, who ruled over the underworld. However, he corrects the popular belief that the god of the dead remains under the earth. On the contrary, this god (Hades, Pluto or Osiris) is far removed from the earth and matter; Plutarch thinks that the souls of the dead rise to the invisible and eternal realm of this God, for whose ineffable beauty they have always longed. There he will then be their ruler and king.[4]

Plutarch interprets the role of Isis as that of bringing human beings to the *gnosis* of the one who is the First and the Lord. Isis issues a call to seek this highest God; thus she herself also always lives in communion with him. Plutarch gives an apt explanation of Isis' name; he connects it with the Greek word for 'know'. He explains that the name of Isis' temple in Delphi, Iseion, promises *gnosis* of the true reality. Thus according to Plutarch the name Isis means knowledge.[5]

As a Platonic philosopher Plutarch seems to be able to interpret Isis as the goddess who gives knowledge of the highest God. For him Osiris is one of the designations of the first God in heaven, to whom the souls who have received the true knowledge will rise after the death of the body. He did not regard the worship of Isis as being in competition with his own service of Apollo. He was on good terms with the priestess Clea, who had been initiated into the mysteries of Isis and Osiris, and to whom he had dedicated this book.[6] Plutarch seems to be able to fit this Egyptian myth perfectly into his own religious philosophy.

1.2. Apuleius of Madaura on the worship of Isis and Osiris

Although Plutarch gives a good insight into the myth of Isis and Osiris, he does not show any deep piety towards Isis. From the many pieces of evidence of this piety I have chosen the book *Metamorphoses*, which the Middle Platonist

Apuleius of Madaura (in North Africa) wrote in Latin in the second century.

The main character of the book is called Lucius.[7] By magic he had unfortunately been changed into an ass.[8] In this guise he had had numerous dangerous adventures. Finally one night, at full moon, he arrived at Cenchreae, near Corinth. There he immersed his head seven times in the sea and when speaking the names of a number of goddesses invoked the moon as the queen of heaven. Then 'queen Isis' appeared to him under her true name. She promised him redemption from his fate, and her powerful protection. He had to put his life totally at her service and live a chaste life: 'Then you will *know* that I – and I alone – can even prolong your life beyond the limits determined by your fate' (XI, 1–6).[9]

The next day, as Isis had foretold to him, a procession of her adherents came by. When Lucius joined it and ate the garland of roses that the priest held out, he changed back from an ass into a human being. Isis had already prepared the priest in the procession for this. He stated that anyone who devotes himself completely to Isis need no longer fear the fate that is expressed in robbers, wild animals, dangerous journeys and the daily fear of death. The priest taught him that if he accepted the yoke of service to Isis willingly, he would experience freedom as its fruit (XI,7–15).

Those in the procession said that Lucius was reborn. Others regarded him as having returned from the realm of the dead. After a preparatory period of prayer, fasting and a cleansing in water, Lucius was consecrated to the service of Isis in a secret rite. He received an appropriate garment and took part in a solemn meal. In a devout prayer he praised Isis as the most powerful goddess of the world, the stars and all the gods (XI, 16–25).

On the instructions of Isis Lucius went to Rome, where he was to serve in her temple. There she made it known to him that he would be initiated again, into the service of Osiris, 'the great God and Father of all the gods'. And so it happened. Then followed a third initiation, after which Osiris himself appeared personally to him as the most high God. In this vision Osiris made it known to him that he might enter the highest priestly order (XI, 26–30).

Apuleius's book, which is largely written as an adventure story, thus has an extremely serious conclusion. But religious questions occur throughout the book, however comic and exciting the way in which Lucius' vicissitudes are described. However humorous the description, the book is always about the threat of magic and inescapable fate. The power of the traditional gods and goddesses is put in question, itinerant priests who go on mission for the Syrian mother goddess are mocked for their sexual abuse of a youth and their greed for money; and a woman who calls her god 'the Only one' (Christ?) is depicted as a cunning adulteress.[10] Finally Isis proves to be the true goddess who surpasses all gods and powers, including magic and fate. She alone gives access to Osiris, the most high God.

In this book Lucius is an example of the person who initially devotes himself to reckless adventures and sexual desires, but in the end finds the truth in the chaste service of Isis. Thus this book contains religious propaganda in novellistic garb. As a background to gnosticism, Apuleius' *Metamorphoses* gives a good picture of the religious quest that a certain category of people undertook at that time.

2. Early Christianity

2.1. Jesus of Nazareth, Son of God

Christianity is one of the new religions which found a following in the Hellenistic world of that time. In my discussion of it I shall assume that the New Testament, which contains the earliest testimonies of faith in Jesus, is reasonably well known. I shall leave aside the question how far the various descriptions in the different Gospels are historically correct; the question is now that of the belief of Christians in the first century of our era.[11]

Christianity – historically speaking – goes back to Jesus of Nazareth. Some years before the beginning of our era he was born of a Jewish mother, Mary. Joseph was regarded as his father, but according to the Gospels of Matthew and Luke he was really fathered by the holy Spirit and God is his true Father. Therefore he is called 'the Son of God'. This God is the God of Abraham, Isaac and Jacob, of Moses and Israel's prophets, the Creator of heaven and earth; this God is addressed by Jesus as 'Father'.[12]

When Jesus was around thirty he began to appear in Galilee as a teacher and prophet. He preached the coming of God's kingdom, forgave people their sins, healed the sick and drove out demons. He gave a radical interpretation of the law of Moses and the prophets, at the centre of which he put devotion and love of God and neighbour. When he came upon unwillingness and unbelief he could threaten people with a sharp judgment.[13] He accused Jewish legal experts of having taken away 'the key of knowledge';[14] by this knowledge (*gnosis* in Greek) he meant knowledge of God and insight into the law of Moses.

Jesus gathered a group of disciples around him and gained much sympathy. But in Jerusalem, with the complicity of the Jewish leaders and the Roman authorities, he was arrested, and after a hastily arranged trial he was crucified.[15] According to the Gospels, Jesus had prepared his disciples for his death and foretold that he would rise from the dead. Although they did not expect this, they did experience that Jesus was alive again on the third day after his crucifixion.[16]

Jesus' death on the cross was regarded as an atoning death which annulled the sins of humankind. This reconciliation with God comes from God the Father himself.[17] Jesus' body after his resurrection from the dead is described in an ambiguous way. On the one hand he appears and disappears like an angel or spirit, suddenly through closed doors, and on the other hand it is attested that his body had flesh and bones again and that he ate baked fish.[18]

The whole of Jesus' life, death and resurrection is described as a fulfilment of dozens of Old Testament prophecies.[19] Both during his lifetime and after his resurrection all kinds of Jewish titles are attributed to him. As well as 'Son of God' he is called Messiah or Christ; both of these mean 'anointed' and point to an expected liberator. The title Son of man points to a heavenly figure with divine authority.[20] The shortest confession is 'Jesus is Lord'.[21] He is identified as the divine Word (*logos*) that has become flesh (or mortal man).[22] People confessed that he had been sent by God from heaven and after his death and resurrection had returned to heaven.[23] From there he was expected back to raise the dead and establish God's kingdom.[24] At the same time the expectation arose that the believers who died before this time would be taken up to Christ in heaven.[25]

2.2. *The dissemination of faith in Jesus Christ*

Jesus' followers experienced that after his resurrection and ascension into heaven they received the Spirit of which he had been full. Their witness to his life and teaching, death and resurrection, aroused faith and gained followers. Thus there arose in Jerusalem and outside groups which believed in Jesus as the Messiah who had come and would return from heaven as Redeemer in order to complete his work.[26]

Not only did Jews come to this faith in Jesus, but also people from other backgrounds. After a number of years the question arose whether these non-Jews (also called 'Gentiles') had to observe the law of Moses in order to be able to join the followers of Jesus Christ. In other words, did they first have to become Jews in order to be able to become Christians, or did they have direct access to Jesus and thus to the God of Israel? Did 'Gentiles' have to observe the regulations for circumcision, the food laws, the laws of cleanness, the observance of the sabbath and the Jewish festivals – or not? If people from other backgrounds did not need first to convert to Judaism in order to be able to become Christians, that would mean that for them Jesus was the access to the God of Israel. But in that

case the earliest Christian communities risked stepping outside the bounds of Judaism.[27]

Paul of Tarsus was the best known champion of the
tendency to release from the complete observance of the law
of Moses people from other backgrounds who had come to
believe in Jesus. He thought that through the death of Jesus
Christ both Jews and Gentiles had been reconciled with God.
According to him the difference between the two groups had
disappeared. Paul thought that it was not necessary for anyone who wanted to join the Christian community to observe
the law of Moses strictly. In his view the only condition was
faith in Jesus Christ as the Lord. Anyone who believed this
had to be baptized in Jesus Christ in order thus to receive the
holy Spirit and to be able to lead a new life.[28]

Of course this view of a Christianity without strict observance of the law of Moses provoked resistance,[29] but in the
second half of the first century it gained the upper hand. The
result was that Christianity acquired adherents who were
Greek or Roman, people from Asia Minor, Syria and Egypt.
These people were less familiar with Judaism. For them Jesus
was the divine teacher and Redeemer who gave them the sight
of God. For these believers from the Gentiles it was not of
primary importance that the God of Jesus was the God of
Israel. They read the Old Testament, but were inclined to
interpret it allegorically or 'spiritually' with reference to Jesus
and the Christian community.

In some cases the link with the Jewish background and the
Jewish observance of the law was cherished.[30] However, those
Christians who had less affinity with the Jewish past or said
good-bye to it because they thought it outdated had greater
influence.[31] Thus at the end of the first century of our era
Christianity fanned out in different directions.

2.3. *Faith in Jesus Christ as the true knowledge*

It was in line with the Judaism and the Hellenistic world in
which earliest Christianity put down roots that Christians
also spoke of 'knowledge' of God and of Christ. Paul openly

uses the term *gnosis*, although he also reacts critically to Christians who referred to their own *gnosis*.[32] Of these he writes: '*gnosis* leads to arrogance'.[33] The First Letter to Timothy (6.20) even warns explicitly against '*gnosis* wrongly so called'. But in general, in the New Testament and in other early Christian literature *gnosis* is a term which could be used directly of Christian faith.[34]

The term *gnosis* does not occur in the Gospel of John, but there is often emphatic mention of knowing (*ginōskein*) God. The conversation between Jesus and his disciple Thomas is typical. When Thomas asks, 'How can we know the way?', Jesus answers:

> I am the way, and the truth, and the life; no one comes to the Father, but by me. If you had known me, you would have known my Father also; henceforth you know him and have seen him.[35]

From this formulation it is evident that the evangelist regarded faith in Jesus Christ as the answer for people who were looking for the way which leads to the true knowledge of God. Anyone who believed in Jesus Christ as the Son of God would receive 'eternal life'. This eternal life is described in the Gospel of John as knowing the only true God and Jesus Christ.[36]

Part III A closer look at gnosticism

9

A form of Hellenized Christianity

Thus far I have reviewed a great many ancient texts from the Hellenistic world with different views of life. In Part I these were a number of myths and texts which are usually called 'gnostic'; in Part II there followed texts of primarily Jewish and Platonic origin. Finally we also discussed earliest Christianity.

The present chapter sets out to bring together this great multiplicity of texts and the views expressed in them. Here the key question is the relationship of the gnostic texts to the Judaism, Christianity and Middle Platonism of this time (I shall usually call this Middle Platonism Platonism). I shall also go more closely into the terms 'gnosis', 'gnostic' and 'gnosticism'.

1. The highest God, the Creator and the world

It is a characteristic of the 'gnostic' texts in Chapters 2 and 4 that the highest God is elevated so high above the material world that he is not regarded as its Creator. Let me recall several facts from these chapters.

In the myth about Simon the Magician, the most high God had the 'thought' of creating angels and archangels, but this 'First Thought' – also called 'Mother of all' – detached herself from him. She then began to create these angels on her own initiative. These angels created the world and imprisoned their Mother, the 'First Thought', in a human body. The Old Testament law and prophets came from these angels.

Menander's doctrine of redemption spoke of an unknown first power and again of a 'Thought'. Menander, too, thought that this Thought had produced angels who had then created the world.

Satornilus, who spoke of an unknown Father who created angels and powers – now without the intermediary of a 'Thought' – is related to this. Seven of these angels created the world and human beings. One of these angels was the God of the Jews.

The Secret Book of John is more complicated, but its structure is related to these three myths. According to this book there is a highly exalted Father from whom the Mother came; among other things she is called 'First Thought'. After the origin of many other heavenly powers, an ugly misbirth, Yaldabaoth, sprang forth from one of them, the disobedient and lustful Sophia (Wisdom). This Yaldabaoth corresponds to the God of the Old Testament. He created his own angels and heavenly spheres and along with his angels created the human being. The human being first consisted of soul substance, but ultimately assumed a material body.

While the passwords from the First Revelation of James and the Ophites offered no developed view of the beginning of creation, they did speak of a most high or pre-existent Father. Yaldabaoth and the frontier guards of the planets were one or more ranks lower.

The overall structure of the doctrine of creation in these myths is as follows. There is a most high unknown Father-God from whom – in most cases – a female figure emerges. This female force is called 'First Thought', 'Mother of all', 'Mother of all things' or 'Mother'. Then there is talk of Sophia, of Wisdom. From this Thought, or from Sophia, after she has removed herself of her own accord from the highest God, proceed the angels who have created the world. This creation of the world and also of the human being is thus not the work, far less the purpose, of the highest Father God.

In the case of Satornilus it is also related how seven angels began to create the world without any mention of a female figure above them. However, their creation of the human being was far from successful.

In the next section I shall investigate the creation of the human being; now we are concerned with the structure of the doctrine of creation in these 'gnostic' myths and its origin. Moreover this structure can be found in all kinds of other 'gnostic' texts.

After the discussion of Plato, Middle Platonism and the Jewish religion, different elements emerged. In the Platonism of this time a distinction was made between the first, most high God, the second God who is called Creator and Lawgiver, and the young gods. Even the Jew Philo seems to be influenced by these distinctions. This Platonic structure can also be seen in the 'gnostic' myths. A feature common to Platonism and the gnostic myths is that the most high God does not get involved as Creator with the material creation, but lower powers are responsible for this. In Plato this is the Creator or the demiurge who created the stars, the planets and the earth from existing material. The Creator left the creation of human bodies to his children, the young gods, while he himself was responsible for the human souls. This Creator and the young gods reappear in the gnostic myths which we have discussed as the creator angelic powers who possibly had a Creator above them. However, one difference is that there is no mention in Platonism that there was a break between the highest God and the creator gods and powers, as is the case in all kinds of 'gnostic' myths.

The 'forms' or 'ideas', which are to be regarded as the model developed by the highest God for the world that was to be formed, are typical of Platonism. These ideas are as it were the thoughts of the highest God, which guided the (lower) Creator in creating the material world. This structure recurs in the gnostic myths in different ways. In a simple form these ideas can be recognized in the 'First Thought' of the highest God according to the Simonians. In a more developed form we meet a parallel with Platonic ideas in the Secret Book of John. It speaks of numerous emanations from the Father, such as the Mother, the Son, lights, aeons, and the heavenly Adam and Seth. In gnostic understanding, this heaven, exalted high above matter, is to be regarded as the world which was really meant by the highest God, and is thus comparable with the higher world of the Platonic ideas.

According to various gnostic myths, the 'First Thought' was responsible for the origin of the creator angels. As I remarked in my discussion of Simon the Magician, the Greek goddess Athene is also called 'the first thought' of her father Zeus, since according to a myth she had arisen from his head. However, according to the Secret Book of John it was not the 'First Thought' but 'Sophia' who was the cause of the origin of the lower angelic powers, contrary to the intention of the Father. This Sophia is to be derived from the Old Testament, where she is a heavenly figure alongside God, who was involved in the creation of the world. Philo even calls her the Mother of the whole creation. But although the Sophia of the Gnostic myths is to be derived from the Old Testament, there is also an important difference from the Old Testament and Judaism around the beginning of our era. The view that Sophia distanced herself from God and thus set about the unintended creation of the material world cannot be found there. This is a new 'gnostic' notion of things, which is thus only in its beginnings derived from the Old Testament and Judaism.[1]

This myth of the fallen Sophia was these gnostics' answer to the question where our so imperfect world comes from. They did not answer this question by pointing to Eve and Adam, who had eaten of the forbidden fruit in paradise, or by pointing to the fall of Satan who was opposed to God. For these gnostics, the cause of the origin of this world with its suffering and misery lay in Sophia. They thought that she had detached herself from the Father and had begun by herself to create angels, who in their turn had begun to create the imperfect world. So in this view the earth is not the creation of the good God who 'saw that it was good', even 'very good' (Gen. 1.31). By contrast, the earth emerges from a fall in the heavenly world. So the evil in the world is given with the creation of the material world. In the next section I shall go into the position of the human being in this imperfect creation.

Gnostics connected the Creator and the angelic creator powers which emerged from the First Thought or Sophia with the Old Testament God the Creator and his powers. This is evident from the Hebrew divine names which this Creator and his angels bore, like Yaldabaoth,[2] Yao, Eloaios, Adonaios, Adoni and Sabbataios. One good reason for identifying this second God, the demiurge of Platonism, with the Old Testament Creator must have been that this second God is regarded not only as Creator but also as Lawgiver. In Plato this Creator makes human souls familiar with the laws of fate before they descend into the material bodies on earth. In Alcinous and Numenius he is therefore also called Lawgiver. Gnostics could connect this designation with the law which Moses received from the Lord God (*yahweh/adonai elohim*) according to the Old Testament.[3]

2. *The creation of human beings*

The Secret Book of John teaches in connection with the creation of the human being that first the heavenly Adam or the true human being emerged from some aeons. Only later, after the abortion of Yaldabaoth from Sophia and his creation of his own angels, is there mention of the creation of Adam's soul-body and, later, of his material body. It is thus imagined that the seven archons began to imitate this 'image' on the basis of the 'likeness' of the highest Father in human form. Here they spoke the words from Gen. 1.26, 'Let us make a human being after the image of God and after the likeness'. They created an Adam of soul substance, but they could not set him on his feet. At the request of Sophia and through a stratagem of the aeon Christ, Yaldabaoth blew the power of the Father into this Adam, so that he began to move. Because the seven angels become jealous of Adam, since by virtue of this power he was more understanding than they, they bound him to a material body on earth. This creation myth is to be found in a much simpler form in Satornilus.

The heavenly Adam who had originally arisen from the aeons is to be regarded as a sort of Platonic 'idea' of the human being which is later worked out in a concrete and material way by the lower gods or angels. Philo, too, spoke of a double creation of the human being, first of his spirit and later of his body.

Within the framework of this Platonic structure, the gnostic myth is an elaboration of the Old Testament notion that the human being is created in God's image and likeness. In the Secret Book of John this heavenly 'image of God' is called both 'human being' and 'son of man'. Here there seems to be a connection with the Jewish tradition that a man or son of man sat on God's throne. According to gnostic ideas this man or son of man was exalted in rank above the Old Testament creator Yaldabaoth.

The Adam that the angels had created then received the power of the Father, the highest God, within him. In the Secret Book of John this power is called 'spirit' (*pneuma*), while Satornilus speaks of the 'spark of life'. That this divine power comes from the most high God, although it is blown into the human being by the Creator Yaldabaoth, is again Platonic. According to Alcinous and Numenius, human souls had come from the most high God, while the second God, the Creator, saw to it that these souls ended up in human beings.

Thus this gnostic myth about the creation of the human being appears to be constructed of both Platonic and Jewish elements. However, the difference from Platonism is that in the gnostic myths the angels have received no commission from the highest God to begin to create the earthly human being. Indeed, their attempt cannot be said to have been successful. Still, the gracious intervention of the most high God who gave his life-force so that the earthly human beings could be capable of life is inspired by Platonism.

The gnostic view that the human being is created on earth in the first instance by lower angelic powers with dubious intentions has important consequences. It follows from this that the human being, to use the words of the Valentinian Theodotus, is thrown into this world. According to the Old Testament creation story, Adam and Eve are put in a paradise from which they are driven by their own fault; they had become guilty of transgressing God's commandment. The gnostic view is quite different. This implies that human beings are victims of the fall which took place earlier in the heavenly world. Indeed, the human being bears no blame for the fact that he lives in this imperfect world; rather, his earthly existence must be said to be tragic. Thus the human being is acquitted of his initial guilt. This element was doubtless attractive compared with the tenor of the Old Testament creation narrative.

3. The Redeemer and the redemption of human beings

According to the Platonic-gnostic notion, the human being thus consists of a transitory body and a nucleus which is not transitory; this nucleus can be called 'spark of life', 'spirit', 'force' or also 'soul'. I shall now call this divine nucleus 'soul'. In the texts we have discussed, the fate of the soul is described in different ways. Among the Simonians Helen is regarded as the prototype of the human being who is imprisoned in material existence and is doomed to ever new reincarnations until she encounters the Redeemer in Simon. Through the knowledge of Simon, or through the grace of the highest God, she is redeemed from this cycle of reincarnations. In the Exegesis on the Soul the soul comes to repent and tries to break with her adulterous existence. The theme of reincarnation did not recur there, nor did it in the other gnostic texts discussed. Reincarnation is even denied in the Secret Book of John. In so far as this theme does occur in gnostic texts, this element can be derived from Platonism.[4]

In the gnostic myths, mention is made in different ways

of a Redeemer who has descended from heaven. For the Simonians this was Simon, but they also recognized Jesus and the holy Spirit. Menander regarded himself as Redeemer. In the Exegesis on the Soul, the Redeemer was a heavenly bridegroom-brother who speaks words that appear in the New Testament in the mouth of Christ. For Satornilus Christ was the Redeemer. The Redeemer is also called Christ in the Secret Book of John, but at the end, at the same time it is said that the Mother descended to the earth three times to make the redemption known.

According to some texts this redemption consists in the acquisition of knowledge. That is the case with the Simonians, Menander and the Secret Book of John. The Exegesis on the Soul speaks of the recognition of the bridegroom-brother and the recollection of the Father's house. Satornilus, – at least in Irenaeus's brief account – did not speak of knowledge but of trust in Christ. This does not mean that he cannot also have spoken of 'knowledge'. This knowledge (or gnosis) gives insight into the origin and destiny of the soul. Redemption through knowledge or recollection is regarded as a divine grace. Sometimes (as with the Simonians and in the Exegesis on the Soul) it is explicitly stated that this grace cannot be earned by righteous works or asceticism. However, it is said that Satornilus practised an ascetic life-style.

Through the revelation of the true knowledge and conversion to the highest God, as a human being one can thus learn what life is about. One can learn where one's soul comes from, how to live a pure life in accord with this divine nucleus, and where the soul goes after the death of the body. According to gnostic insight the destiny of the soul lies above the heavenly spheres of the planets and their powers, near to the true and most high God. Learning the correct passwords to get past the archons on the planets could be part of the redemptive knowledge. Above all in the Exegesis on the Soul, which speaks of recognizing and recalling, it becomes clear that this vision is Platonic. According to Platonism the soul comes from the starry heaven and it is its destiny to recall this origin during its life on earth and to return to it after the death of the body.

Since redemption consists of conversion to true knowledge, the Redeemer has the function of a heavenly teacher who reveals this knowledge. In various of the texts discussed this teacher is called Christ. This is an important Christian element. By comparison with the New Testament it is striking that in these gnostic texts redemption is not based on the death and resurrection of Christ. The Secret Book of John relates only that he has returned whence he came. In the myth of Simon the Magician it is denied that the Redeemer really suffered in Judaea. In Satornilus the Redeemer is described by the Platonic terms 'unbegotten', 'incorporeal' and 'without form'. In the Exegesis on the Soul the bridegroom-brother (who speaks words of Christ) similarly does not have the features of a human being of flesh and blood.

Thus in these gnostic myths Christ is characterized above all as a heavenly teacher and not as the one who through his death and resurrection brings about redemption for human-kind from sin and death. The reason why the gnostics mostly did not acknowledge this is not that they already held the modern theological view that the significance of Jesus lies in his emergence as an exceptional Jewish rabbi and prophet. The gnostic view of Christ as a heavenly teacher is to be explained from the Platonic structure of these myths. Christ (or whatever other redeemer) is regarded as sent by the highest God and not by the Creator, the God of the Jews. From the perspective of the highest God, life in an earthly body is an unintended consequence of a dramatic fall from his high heaven. These myths are about the redemption of the divine souls which the highest God has put in human beings on earth so that they recall their high origin. Because, in their view, the Redeemer is an emissary of the highest God and not of the Creator, some unclarity remains about the bodily exist-ence of this Redeemer. Since he is descended from the highest God, his bodily nature – in contrast to the New Testament – is of subordinate importance or really unwanted or even impossible. Along these lines Christ's bodily death and his resurrection from the dead was irrelevant or even inconceivable for a number of 'gnostics'.[5]

As already emerged, another aspect of this view is that Christ does not derive from the God of the Old Testament. Satornilus in fact taught explicitly that Christ wanted to destroy the God of the Jews. Thus Jesus Christ is detached from his Jewish and Old Testament background.

4. *Gnostics, the Old Testament and creation*

The attitude of gnostics towards the Old Testament varies: this is also evident from the texts which are discussed in Part I. The Simonians and Satornilus thought that the Old Testament was inspired by the lower angels who had created the world, or even partly by Satan. Indeed the Simonians argued that the Old Testament commandments would lead to slavery. In the Exegesis on the Soul, by contrast, the Old Testament is quoted as inspired by the holy Spirit, and not for example by the 'robbers' who held the soul prisoner. Various Old Testament books (Genesis, prophets and psalms) were regularly related in a spiritual sense to the state of the soul.[6] The Old Testament functions in quite a different way in the Secret Book of John. In it, all kinds of elements from the first chapters of Genesis and other texts are used and interpreted. Thus the jealous Yaldabaoth, who thinks that he is the only God and who has created the lower angelic powers, and, together with them, the material world, is far below the highest Father God in rank. It becomes clear from this that in this gnostic version the biblical creation narrative has come to stand in another framework, which is akin to that of Satornilus and the Simonians. But the Secret Book of John does not turn against the Old Testament as such; it is only used in a quite distinctive way.[7] It is already clear from what has been said above that many elements of this gnostic usage are to be derived from Platonism.

If this world is regarded as a creation of a lower God or of still lower angelic powers, the result can be that life in the earthly body is seen above all in a negative light. In any case the most high God has then – according to this view – not given bodily life on earth; only the soul in the body comes from him. Certainly the highest God's concern for the earth according to the gnostic myths emerges from the fact that he sends a Redeemer to earth from his heaven in order to reveal the true knowledge.

It has often been thought that because of their view of the world, gnostics in fact took a very negative view of life on earth. Therefore there is talk of their anti-cosmic attitude. Life in this world (*kosmos*) is said to be only a caprice of a Creator who arose from the First Thought or Sophia as an abortion. However, it is important to explain the gnostic pattern in the first place as a radical Platonism which was applied to early Christianity (or to another religion) by people who already thought in Platonic terms. In Platonism it was customary to make a distinction between the highest God and the lower Creator, and between the immortal soul from heaven and the body which was thought to be inferior. But these traditional distinctions did not *per se* mean that people who thought in Platonic terms did not feel absolutely at home on earth. Like everyone else, they had to suffer under fates like sickness, sorrow, violence and death. The Platonic knowledge of the higher world to which the soul that had lived virtuously could return after the death of the body offered them a comforting answer to the great questions of life.

Indeed many gnostics had a more negative view of the Creator and his creator than was customary in Platonic philosophy. It is from this that the view mentioned above that gnostics usually showed contempt for the world in their behaviour is derived. This attitude could then result either in strict asceticism or in sexual licentiousness. But the original 'gnostic' texts give little or no occasion for this conclusion;[8] indeed it is based especially on texts from the church fathers and the philosopher Plotinus, who fought against the gnostics.[9] It is true that a low view of life in this world and in the human body was to be found among gnostics; but this was equally the case among catholic Christians from this time.[10] It has to be said that this alleged loose-living can occur among certain gnostics as a consequence of their view of the world. But the possibility that this accusation is based on slander cannot be excluded. The catholic Christians, too, were regularly accused of being immoral, but that is no reason to assume that this mud-slinging was justified.[11]

This moderate view of the gnostics raises the question why the Old Testament Creator is often portrayed in such a negative way in their myths, so that his creation is also judged to be a failure. The often negative gnostic attitude to the Old Testament can be explained from all those passages which were offensive to Hellenistic readers. I have already presented some critical questions about the image of God in the first chapters of Genesis (pp. 68f.). But for those who begin to read the Old Testament unprepared, there are far more parts which give the impression that the Lord is a mediocre or even terrifying God. The prophetic preaching of judgment causes dismay, indeed fear and aversion. The fact that the Lord is compared with a devouring lion[12] means that he himself does not live up to the Platonic image of the (lower) Creator from the *Timaeus*, who is only good and is not responsible for evil. Moreover it is said in the name of the Lord that he is jealous,[13] and that there is no God beside him.[14] If this Lord is the Creator, then – the judgment of Hellenistic readers could be – he is an untrustworthy and arrogant Creator.[15]

People who felt attracted to Christianity and encountered such 'gnostic' views will in many cases already have been thinking in Platonic terms before they came into contact with the Christian faith. Since they could not give up their Platonic view of the world, they integrated their philosophy into the Christian religion.[16] In the Christian communities they came upon the Old Testament – if they did not know it already – to which catholic Christians attributed a divine authority. However, the image of the Lord God that emerged from it raised all kinds of critical questions for interested parties or converts. These questions were whether this Lord God had not acted cruelly and arbitrarily towards humankind and thus whether he was completely good. Christians with a Platonic background could partly answer these critical questions by not identifying the Lord God of the Old Testament with the highest God but with the lower Creator from Platonism. Because of the doubtful impression made by the Old Testament God on these readers with a Platonic background, they described him as Creator in even more negative terms than the Creator of Platonic philosophy. That explains to a large degree the origin of myths like those of Satornilus and the Secret Book of John.

It is possible that such radical Platonizing interpretations of the Old Testament already existed in Jewish circles.[17] Thus it is said that the Secret Book of John seems to have been Christianized only at a second stage. If all the Christian elements are removed as later additions, what remains is a Jewish gnostic myth.[18] There is no mistaking the fact that Philo used Platonism, albeit in a less dualistic form, for his exposition of the Septuagint. In any case it can be concluded that the gnostics who interpreted the Old Testament in accordance with a dualistic Platonic pattern also knew Jewish traditions and used them in their myths.

This specifically 'gnostic' interpretation of the Old Testament – this *gnosis* – also attracted believers who did not have a Platonic background.[19] The gnostic myths and interpretations offered all kinds of answers to the difficult questions about the Old Testament which Hellenistic readers could raise.

It is evident from the warnings of the church fathers that these gnostics sometimes formed part of the catholic communities.[20] However, where the bishop and other leaders of a community could not tolerate the gnostic views, there was a split. This gave rise to separate catholic and gnostic communities, each of which had its own meetings and rituals. Origen describes this origin of separate trends or sects in his work against Celsus, offering some excuses. He then goes into

Celsus' criticism that Christianity consisted of so many different trends which disputed one another, and writes:

> So then, since Christianity appeared to men as something worthy of serious attention, not only to people of the lower classes as Celsus thinks, but also to many scholars among the Greeks, sects (*haireseis*) inevitably came to exist, not at all on account of factions and love of strife, but because several learned men made a serious attempt to understand the doctrines of Christianity. The result of this was that they interpreted differently the scriptures universally believed to be divine, and sects arose named after those who, although they admired the origin of the Word, were impelled by certain reasons which convinced them to disagree with one another.[21]

5. The Platonizing of Hellenistic religions

In § 3 it proved that Christ appeared as the Redeemer in various 'gnostic' myths. In a Platonic way he is regarded as an emissary from the highest God and not from the Creator God of the Old Testament, who is thought to be lower. The view that Christ as Redeemer comes from the highest God and not from the Old Testament God can be regarded as a form of Platonizing of Christianity. The Christian faith is interpreted in the Platonic categories of a higher and a lower God.

Early Christianity is not the only religion to have undergone such Platonizing. Another example already emerged in our discussion of Philo. In Chapter 7.2.6 I concluded that Philo is a witness both to Platonism and to the Hellenizing of the Jewish religion. If we take these two types together, then we can speak of Philo's Platonizing of Judaism.[22]

A similar process of of Platonizing can be recognized in the worship of Simon the Magician. According to the New Testament book of the Acts of the Apostles he was known in Samaria as 'the great power of God', and he could perform miracles. Later, too, in the second century, there appears to have been a group which worshipped Simon. The 'myth' or 'doctrine' about Simon underwent some changes at that time. He was then regarded as the incarnation of the highest God and people spoke of his 'First Thought' which had produced angels and powers that had then created the world. The angels had compelled this First Thought to reincarnate from one body to another. Some Platonic elements come out clearly here. There is a good highest God; his 'Thought' suggests the 'ideas'; there are lower creator powers; and there is a heavenly soul which is doomed to reincarnation. Not everything can be explained from Platonism; thus the incarnation of this highest God in Simon cannot be derived directly from it. Certainly at that time people believed that gods could descend in human form; probably, however, the Simonians wanted above all to offer an alternative to the Christian view that God has become human in Jesus Christ. This does not alter the fact that the Platonic pattern can be recognized clearly among the Simonians. Thus we can speak of a Platonizing of the original (first-century) worship of Simon as the 'great power of God'.

Another example of Platonizing can be seen in the worship of Isis and Osiris. The two witnesses to this mystery religion that I have discussed, Plutarch and Apuleius, were both Platonic philosophers. Plutarch appears to be able to explain the Egyptian myth about the divine pair in terms of the highest God, Osiris, and the 'ideas' of the creation which Isis had received. As Redeemer, Isis offers the true knowledge of the highest God, to whom souls may rise after the death of the body. This distinction between Osiris and Isis returns in a comparable way in Apuleius. Although their interpretation cannot be explained completely in terms of Platonism, the influence of this philosophy can be clearly recognized – which is not surprising in two Platonic philosophers. Thus this is the fourth example of the Platonizing of a religion to have occurred in the Hellenistic world.

More examples of this could be given, like the Hermetic literature (from the first centuries of our era) in which Hermes has a central place. In Greek mythology Hermes was the messenger of the gods and the guide of souls to the underworld. In the Hermetic texts, on the one hand he is presented as the person who can initiate others into Egyptian wisdom and knowledge, and on the other as the god who corresponds with the Egyptian god Thoth, the Creator. But in the Hermetic texts a distinction is also made between a first God and a second God, the Creator.[23] Moreover Hermetic texts contain various Old Testament motifs. The Hermetic doctrine of life – also called *gnosis* – thus has an Egyptian origin; it has incorporated elements from the Old Testament and it is influenced by Platonic philosophy.[24]

It will be clear that early Christianity has its place in this series of examples of the Platonizing of Hellenistic religions. The Platonizing of Christianity took place in all kinds of ways and to different degrees. 'Catholic' church fathers too made use of Platonic terms and notions.[25] A radical form of Platonizing of Christianity is to be found in the literature that is usually called 'gnostic'. We shall now look more closely at the terms gnosis, gnostic and gnosticism.

6. *What is gnosis, what is a gnostic and what is gnosticism?*

So far I have used the terms 'gnosis', 'gnostic', and 'gnosticism' as they are generally used in scholarly and popular scholarly terminology. However, in Chapter 1 I already indicated that the use of these designations is not a matter of course.

In 1966 a congress was held in Messina in Italy at which those present proposed that the following distinction should be made between the terms 'gnosis' and 'gnosticism'. 'Gnosis' should in general denote knowledge of the divine mysteries, which is reserved for an elite. By contrast, 'gnosticism' should be understood to denote particular systems from the second century which have the following characteristics in common. Human beings are said to have a divine spark in them which derives from the heavenly world but has fallen into this world of misery, birth and death. By a call or revelation from the high heavenly world this spark must be brought to life again. To this corresponds a fall of Sophia or Thought from the divine world, which indirectly gave rise to the material world. To the degree that the origin of this world (*kosmos*) is regarded in the gnostic systems as a wrong move, this congress spoke of 'anti-cosmic dualism'. The gnosis of the gnostic was to clarify knowledge of the condition of human beings on earth. So not every form of gnosis could be called 'gnostic', but the gnosis of the gnostics was to teach how the fallen divine spark in human beings can be restored to its original state. The one who teaches this gnosis was to be called a 'gnostic'.[26]

Certainly objections have also been made to these definitions.[27] Thus one objection to the definition of 'gnosis' in terms of gnosticism is that it does not agree with the usage in antiquity. We have seen that the term gnosis for religious or philosophical knowledge occurred in Plato, Philo and Plutarch, in the Septuagint, in the New Testament and in other Jewish and early Christian writers. In Greek, *epistēmē* also regularly occurred as a term for 'knowledge', in Hebrew *da'at*, or the verb 'know', was used for what was essential in living and dying. In a similar way, the term 'knowledge' is also used in the myths of the Simonians, Menander and the Secret Book of John. In general, however, it cannot be said that this knowledge was always reserved for an elite. This aspect did occur in the Secret Book of John and in Satornilus (although there was no mention of 'knowledge' in Irenaeus' account of Satornilus). In the Secret Book of John, however, it did not seem that this knowledge has to remain limited to a particular group. The purpose seemed to be simply that all souls should acquire the true knowledge, possibly after the death of the body. It was only for apostates that the author offered no hope.

One objection to the current use of the term 'gnostic' is that we do not know whether many so-called gnostics called themselves such. The term 'gnostics' occurs above all in some church fathers and in Plotinus, who applied the term to tendencies which in their eyes were heretical and challenged them under this designation.[28] Probably some tendencies will indeed have regarded themselves as 'gnostics', over against the catholic Christians, i.e. as people who had more or deeper knowledge. But even a 'catholic' teacher like Clement of Alexandria used this term for catholic Christians who had made progress over insight and way of life and who did not only believe.[29]

Another objection to the use of the term 'gnostic' according to the Messina definitions is that it is regularly difficult to establish whether or not a writing can be called 'gnostic'. In that case the criteria would be whether the divine spark which has fallen into human beings from the heavenly world appears in it, and whether the lower Creator is distinguished from the highest God. However, it proves that these elements sometimes do not occur in writings which usually tend to be characterized as 'gnostic'. I shall limit myself now to the texts which were discussed in Chapters 2–4. It can be said that the motif of the fallen soul does appear in the Exegesis on the Soul, but not the motif that the world has been created by a lower Creator or by angelic powers. It is therefore even conceivable that this pious sermon could have been given in a catholic community without provoking protests. But there did seem to be an affinity with the other myths from chapters 2 and 4. Thus the 'robbers' of the Exegesis on the Soul appear to be a designation for the lower angelic powers in one of the versions of the Secret Book of John.

Like M. Smith earlier, M. A. Williams has proposed that the term 'gnostic' should no longer be used because it is unclear. As an alternative he introduces the term 'biblical demiurgical traditions'.[30] By demiurgical traditions he understands the traditions which start from a distinction between the highest God and a lower Creator (demiurge) or creators of the world. Since this distinction applies to Platonism generally, he adds the term 'biblical' to make it clear that he is referring to those traditions which contain Jewish or Christian elements. He sees as an advantage of the designation 'biblical demiurgical traditions' that it is at least clearly a modern term. Such a technical term would prevent people from continuing to talk of a 'biblical demiurgical religion', just as they speak of 'the gnostic religion' as though this ever existed as a whole.[31]

There is something to be said for this proposal of Williams'. But the question is whether the established terms 'gnosis', 'gnostic' and 'gnosticism' can be abolished so easily.[32] Despite the objections made to them, I have used them at least in this book because they are known. It is possible to use 'gnosis' and 'gnostic' as global (and modern) designations for those tendencies in antiquity which interpreted an existing religion in a Platonic sense. Dualism in creation is characteristic of this Platonizing. This entails, first, that the God who is responsible for the creation of the earth and the planets is of a much lower status than the highest God who belongs in the world far above the planets. The origin of the lower Creator God is often a consequence of a fall from the heavenly world of the highest God. Secondly, this dualism in creation includes the fact that the body of the human being comes from God the Creator or his fellow-workers, whereas the human being has a divine nucleus which comes from the most high God. A third characteristic of this Platonizing is that people can learn to know the true, highest and good God by recalling the origin of their souls.

If this Platonism has incorporated elements of Judaism and Christianity to a greater or lesser degree, it can – by agreement – be called Christian gnosis or gnosticism. The terms 'gnosis' and 'gnosticism' can then be used indiscriminately. The persons involved here can be called 'gnostics', in accord with the church fathers and Plotinus. But once again, these terms can only be used as global (and modern) designations. The first centuries of our era show a great variety of writings in which Jewish, Christian and Platonic elements are woven into a whole in very different ways. In Chapters 10 and 11

I shall give yet other examples than those which have been discussed at more length in Chapters 2–4. It would be wrong to think that all these writings bear witness to a coherent tendency or religion. The sweeping use of the terms 'gnosis' and 'gnostic' means that it is impossible always to indicate clearly which writings are 'gnostic' and which are not.[33]

Now catholic Christian authors are also sometimes strongly influenced by Platonism, and moreover speak of their gnosis. As I have mentioned, Clement of Alexandria himself calls the advanced Christian a 'gnostic'. However, catholic Christian authors do not teach any dualism in creation; this would make them heretics. Thus catholic Christian gnosis can be recognized by its monism in creation. This means that there is one God who has created heaven and earth and the human soul and the body, and who is the Father of Jesus Christ the Redeemer.

As for Philo, it is certainly possible to speak of his Jewish gnosis.[34] By emphatically maintaining monotheism he proved formally to oppose a dualism in creation, while elements of this can nevertheless be found in his works. This obvious lack of consistency again shows how difficult it is to draw sharp dividing lines. However, it is not customary to call Philo a gnostic.

7. Gnosis as a form of the Hellenization of Christianity

Long before the Nag Hammadi writings were discovered, Adolf von Harnack, who wrote an important history of dogma, characterized gnosticism as the acute secularization or Hellenization of Christianity.[35] By that he meant that already at an early stage the 'gnostics' made use of Hellenistic philosophy to present Christian faith to the culture of the time. Now various of Harnack's views have been made obsolete by the discovery of the Nag Hammadi books. Thus he thought that the gnostics as a rule rejected the Old Testament. His own critical view of the Old Testament and of Judaism may also be said to be suspect.[36] Although it is now clearer how gnostics drew on Jewish traditions, we can still argue that Harnack's characterization of gnosticism as the acute Hellenization of Christianity had touched on the heart of the matter. It has emerged that of this Hellenistic philosophy, Middle Platonism above all was an important ingredient for the gnostic systems. Gnostic Christians were not afraid to integrate Platonic views into the Christian faith that they had come to know. Christ was the emissary of the highest God, the God who is believed alone to be good, and the capricious God of the Old Testament is assigned a second or even lower place. In this way they felt that they were making belief in Christ meaningful for themselves and all those whom they encountered. Thus these gnostic Christians were answering in their own way the great questions of life: How and for what purpose have we come upon earth? What is the cause of evil and suffering? How can we be redeemed from it? What are we to expect after death?

Harnack also gave an apt characterization of catholic Christianity. He said that it had undergone a gradual Hellenization in which the Old Testament was preserved. Catholic leaders and church fathers in fact proved able to hold on to the refractory Old Testament as Holy Scripture for the Christian church. However, by this 'gradual Hellenization' Harnack meant that catholic Christianity, too, did not avoid being influenced by Hellenistic philosophy, but that this Hellenism was accepted in more moderate doses. I shall be giving some examples of this in Chapter 12.

10

Some gnostic and related teachers

The preceding views on gnosticism were mainly based on the selection of evidence about gnostics and gnostic works which had been discussed in chapters 2–4. However, this book would be an all too incomplete introduction to gnosticism were I to limit myself completely to this selection. Therefore in this chapter I shall discuss some gnostic and related teachers who so far have been mentioned only in passing, if at all. Most of these teachers are known above all through the church fathers who have written about them and quoted them. Many of their views will by now seem familiar. Since the backgrounds have already been discussed, they will no longer be introduced in detail.

The works which were found in Nag Hammadi are not relevant here because these are either anonymous or bear the name of people who cannot be the real authors. Some of these writings will come up in the next chapter.

1. Cerinthus

Irenaeus knows of one Cerinthus who taught in Asia Minor that the world was not created by the first God but by a much lower Power who was in ignorance of the highest Power. Cerinthus thought it impossible that Jesus had been born of a virgin: he regarded him on the one hand as the son of Joseph and Mary and on the other as the son of the Creator. He said that Jesus surpassed all human beings in justice, sobriety and wisdom. After Jesus' baptism, Christ had descended on him in the form of a dove: according to Cerinthus this Christ has the supreme Power as Father. It is Christ who made this unknown Father known and did miracles. Finally this Christ flew away from Jesus again. The man Jesus suffered and rose, but Christ remained in his spiritual state, in which he could not suffer.[1]

Hippolytus adds that Cerinthus had received his schooling from the Egpytians.[2] Irenaeus mentions the tradition that when the apostle John saw Cerinthus in the baths at Ephesus he fled unwashed for fear that the baths would collapse: John is then said to have remarked: 'for in them is Cerinthus, the enemy of truth'.[3] According to another tradition this John had written his Gospel to refute the errors of Cerinthus. Irenaeus states that according to this Gospel there is one God, who has created everything by his Word (the *logos*) and through this Word has also given redemption to humankind.[4]

It is uncertain how trustworthy these traditions are. But it can probably be inferred from them that the beginning of Cerinthus' activity fell at the end of the first century. This makes Cerinthus a contemporary of Menander of Antioch.

2. Basilides, Isidorus and the Basilidians

Basilides lived in Alexandria in the first half of the second century. Nothing would be known of his twenty-four books on the gospel and his school had not the church fathers written about them. A number of fragments of his works have been preserved, above all thanks to Clement of Alexandria.[5] It seems from this that Basilides discussed Christian themes like faith, hope, love, sin, election and martyrdom. He quoted and explained texts from the Old and New Testaments. In accord with Platonism he began from a highest good God and a lower ruler of the world, but according to W. A. Löhr he did not set these two gods over against each other. According to various witnesses Basilides taught the possibility of reincarnation. The term gnosis does not occur in the fragments which have been handed down. A great lack in these fragments is that we cannot see from them what view Basilides had of Jesus Christ. He seems to have referred to the secret teaching of the

apostle Matthias and one Glaucius who is called the inter-
preter of Peter.[6]

It is known that among other works his son and disciple
Isidore wrote a book called *Ethica*. From this book there is a
tradition of how Isidore gave advice on marriage, sexual continence and celibacy on the basis of the Gospel of Matthew
(19.11–12) and Paul's first letter to the Corinthians (7.9).[7]

Irenaeus and Hippolytus also wrote about Basilides and his
school, but their evidence is hard to reconcile with that of
Clement. Presumably later disciples reworked his teaching, so
that while it still bore the name of Basilides it did not go back
to him. I shall give only some details of the discussion by
Irenaeus here.[8] According to him, Basilides taught about
many heavenly powers which had made the world. One
of them, the God of the Jews, wanted to subject the other
peoples to the Jews. Because this caused a dispute between
the angelic powers and the peoples, the highest God sent his
only-begotten son, Christ. He appeared on earth in the form
of a man, Jesus, and performed miracles there. He was not
crucified, but Simon of Cyrene was crucified in his place,
while Jesus mocked the angelic powers. He himself ascended
and returned to the Father. According to Irenaeus's account
of Basilides' teaching, anyone who believed in the crucified
Jesus was still a slave of the angels who had made the bodies.
But anyone who denied the crucified Jesus would be freed
from the influence of these angels and learn to know the most
high Father. The Old Testament was inspired by these angels.
There was redemption only for the soul, not for the perishable
body. Irenaeus accuses Basilides' disciples of giving rein to
their desires, of offering sacrifices to idols and of magical
practices. Their teaching was intended only for a few and had
to be kept secret.[9]

These last characteristics, the trustworthiness of which is
difficult to establish, determined the picture that the catholic
church formed of Basilides as a heretic. The fragments which
Clement has handed down in fact confirm that Basilides
distinguished between a highest and a lower God, a view

which is not catholic and orthodox. However, anyone who like Löhr is willing to use only the fragments that have been handed down can possibly arrive at a moderate verdict on Basilides. He can then be put at the beginning of the Alexandrian philosophical Christian tradition which – with all kinds of differences – is continued by Clement and Origen.[10]

3. Valentinus

Since the second century Valentinus has been known as the founder of the gnostic tendency of the Valentinians. Half-way through the second century, for some time he was a prominent member of the catholic community in Rome. Epiphanius reports the tradition that he came from Egypt and had received his schooling in Alexandria. Clement reports that he had been taught by one Theodas, who in turn had been a disciple of the apostle Paul. According to Tertullian Valentinus was very capable and eloquent and in Rome had even hoped for the office of bishop. When he did not attain it he is said to have broken with the catholic church.[11]

A small number of fragments of Valentinus's works consisting of sermons, letters and a hymn have been preserved through Clement of Alexandria and Hippolytus. From these fragments we can infer that Valentinus explained the Old and New Testaments with the help of the philosophy of that time. According to Christoph Markschies, the fragments lacked typically 'gnostic' views, like the distinction between a higher God and a lower, rebellious Creator.[12] We can certainly read here that Adam was created after a heavenly model by angels who were then afraid of him.[13] However, Markschies thinks that this view would also fit into a Platonic context like that to be found in Philo. Valentinus thought that Jesus ate and drank but that the food was not digested; this was said to be a sign of his self-control and his divinity.[14]

In contrast to what seems to be the case from these fragments, Irenaeus attributed to Valentinus a gnostic mythological system with thirty heavenly aeons which together form the 'fullness' (*pleroma*). There is a Mother in it who brings forth Christ and the Creator outside the *pleroma*, but these do not coincide with the man Jesus and the highest Father respectively.[15]

According to Markschies, Irenaeus's information will have come from the later Valentinians, who will have diverged from Valentinus. For this development he refers to some remarks by Tertullian and to various examples from antiquity of disciples who took a different way from their masters.[16] Others think that the reports about Valentinus's gnostic views by church fathers like Irenaeus and Tertullian are more trustworthy.[17]

The fragmentary character of the texts of Valentinus which have been preserved make it difficult to adopt a definitive standpoint on his position. It certainly seems that Valentinus advocated a Christianity with a mystical and philosophical orientation which – again with all the differences – found a following in Clement and Origen. However, the later relationship between the disciples of Valentinus and catholic Christianity was far from warm. Thus Clement writes that the followers of Valentinus regard 'us' (the catholic Christians) as simple people to whom they attribute *faith,* while they think that *gnosis* is in themselves. Through the excellent seed that is to be found in them they are by nature redeemed, and their gnosis is as far removed from faith as the spiritual from the psychical.[18]

4. *Ptolemaeus*

According to Irenaeus, Ptolemaeus was 'a flower from the school of Valentinus'.[19] According to Hippolytus, he belonged to the 'Italian' (Western) tendency of the Valentinians[20] and can be dated to the second half of the second century. Irenaeus offers an extended description of the mythical system of Ptolemaeus, which begins with thirty heavenly aeons. The myth shows an affinity to the Secret Book of John. A completely transcendent Father and a Thought appear in it, and also Christ and the holy Spirit; similarly Sophia, who unintentionally becomes the cause of the origin of the Creator and the creation of the world and humankind. Humankind is divided into the earthy, the psychics and the pneumatics. Those who are only earthy perish. 'Psychics' are to be found in the church; they can be redeemed by good works and by faith, but they lack the spiritual seed and true gnosis. Those who are 'pneumatic' or spiritual are redeemed through their gnosis and the spiritual seed that is in them. Christ had in him a spiritual element from Sophia and a psychic element from the Creator. His 'psychic' body had gone through Mary like water through a tube, and at his baptism the Redeemer had descended on him from on high. However, he had not suffered on the cross because he could not suffer. In support of his views Ptolemaeus quoted a large number of texts from the New Testament and a smaller number from the Old Testament. However, Irenaeus observes that these interpretations do violence to the texts and go against the obvious meaning. He accuses these Valentinians of eating food dedicated to idols and taking part in pagan festivals, animal fights and competitions between gladiators.[21] If this last is correct, it means that they maintained less distance from Roman society than that to which catholic Christians were called.

Irenaeus's description is that of a critical outsider who gives all kinds of information but does not achieve the tone that we would hear from Ptolemaeus himself. However, an original doctrinal letter by Ptolemaeus has been preserved in the work by Epiphanius. In it Ptolemaeus explains to Flora, whom he addresses as 'my dearest sister', how he thinks the Old Testament should be understood. He opposes those who attribute it to the perfect God the Father (as the catholic Christians did) and does not want it to be attributed to the devil either. According to Ptolemaeus, the Old Testament comes partly from the Creator who stands between the perfect God and the devil, partly from Moses and partly from the later Jewish 'elders'. In the part that comes from the Creator himself

Ptolemaeus first distinguishes between the pure lawgiving, like the Ten Commandments, which the Redeemer has come to fulfil; secondly, a less good part which has been abolished by the Redeemer; and thirdly, a symbolic part which must be applied spiritually. In this letter Ptolemaeus does not characterize the Creator in a negative way: he calls him righteous and an image of the highest God. But while he calls the highest God 'perfect', 'unbegotten' and thus eternal, in his view the Creator is 'begotten' and therefore not eternal.[22] So there is no explicit mention here of a break between the highest God and the Creator, but of a hierarchical distinction in accordance with Middle Platonism.

Finally, Ptolemaeus points out that this instruction has a sequel, in which it is explained how all other powers came from the one highest God, including perishability and the Creator. This further teaching presumably corresponds with what Irenaeus has handed down about Ptolemaeus.

5. Heracleon

Like Ptolemaeus, Heracleon is named as an important Valentinian of the 'Italian' tendency;[23] he too appeared in the second half of the second century. In his commentary on the Gospel of John, Origen quotes a large number of fragments of Heracleon's interpretation of this Gospel and discusses them critically. I shall mention only the first fragment here by way of an example.

The first time that Origen quotes Heracleon is in the exposition of John 1.3: 'all things were made by him'. For Origen this means that God the Father has brought everything into existence through the mediation of the Word (*logos*), Christ. However, Heracleon thought that 'all' meant only perishable matter and not the higher world of the divine aeon. According to Heracleon these words mean that the (lower) Creator created the material world because the Logos had appointed him to do this.[24] By the divine aeon Heracleon seems to be pointing to the spiritual world of the highest God, to whom the Logos and the far lower Creator were subordinate.

It regularly proves that Heracleon's exposition of this Gospel is governed by his unorthodox views of God the Father and of the Creator and the creation.

6. *Theodotus*

Theodotus has already been mentioned in Chapter 5, where his questions about gnosis were quoted; there his work was dated around 160–170. According to the superscription of the extracts which Clement of Alexandria made from Theodotus' teaching, Theodotus belonged to the Eastern tendency of the Valentinians. Now Hippolytus tells us that this tendency held the view that the body of Jesus was spiritual and not psychical, as the Italian tendency thought.[25] Clement's extracts teach that Theodotus' view is more complicated: Jesus the Redeemer came from the divine fullness (*pleroma*) and descended to earth clothed with the spiritual seed of Sophia. There he clad himself with the invisible psychic Christ who had been announced in the Old Testament and whom Theodotus calls 'image of the Redeemer'. However, because he needed a visible body, a special body was composed for him in the virgin Mary. The spiritual part of it came from the holy Spirit, according to Luke 1.35a: 'the holy Spirit shall come upon you.' However, the psychic part of this body had come from God the Creator, according to Luke 1.35b: 'the power of the Most High shall overshadow you.'[26]

Thus according to Theodotus, Jesus Christ consisted of four elements. When this body died, the Spirit withdrew from it. The Redeemer raised up this mortal body from the dead, and the psychical Christ sat at the right hand of the Creator. Thus Theodotus attributed a certain redemptive power to the creed of 'psychic' (non-spiritual) catholics. But at the same time he speaks of a higher redemption of all those who believe in a spiritual way.[27]

This exposition, which is sometimes difficult to understand, may serve as an example of Theodotus' teaching. He often quotes texts from the Old and New Testaments in order to support his variant of Valentinian gnosis.

7. *Justin the Gnostic*

Hippolytus describes a system which differs markedly from the other 'gnostic' systems; it is that devised by one Justin.[28] It is unclear when this Justin (not to be confused with Justin Martyr) lived. It has been conjectured that his book, called Baruch, is one of the earliest witnesses to gnosis, but it is safest to date him 'somewhere in the second century'.[29]

According to Justin there were three unbegotten, eternal primal powers, two male and one female. The one male power was the Good, also given the name of the Greek fertility god Priapus; the other was the Father of everything that is begotten in the world: his name was Eloim, which is Hebrew for 'God'. The female power was a virgin with the lower body of an adder; her names were Eden and Israel. Whereas the Good had knowledge of the future, Eloim and Eden lacked this knowledge; they were therefore ignorant. Eloim and Eden made love and produced twenty-four angels who together formed paradise: twelve of them were like their father and twelve like their mother. The angels of Eloim created Adam and Eve, to whom Eden gave the soul and Eloim the spirit (*pneuma*). Adam and Eve received the commandment 'be fruitful and multiply and inherit the earth' (cf. Gen. 1.28).

Hippolytus does not relate precisely how, according to Justin, the heaven and the earth were created. But he does relate that once everything was created, Eloim ascended to the higher parts of heaven to see whether there was still anything lacking in creation. To his amazement he saw at the end of heaven a better light than he himself had created. He could enter it towards the Good and saw 'what no eye has seen, nor ear heard, nor the heart of man conceived' (cf. I Cor. 2.9). He could go and sit on the right hand of the Good (cf. Ps. 110.1), but he wanted to return to the earth to destroy it and to get the spirit of the human being from its body and take it back on high. However, the Good did not allow him.

Eden, who thus had been abandoned by Eloim, commanded her angel Babel or Aphrodite (the Greek goddess of sexuality) to cause adultery and divorce among human beings. Her angel Naas (Hebrew for snake) raped Eve and Adam, which resulted in adultery and pederasty. Thereupon Eloim sent one of his angels (Baruch, Hebrew for 'blessed') to human beings to proclaim the Good so that they should return to him. For that purpose Baruch was sent to Moses, to the prophets and to the Greek hero Heracles, but without success. Finally he was sent to the twelve-year-old shepherd Jesus. Jesus listened to Baruch and led people to know the Father and the Good. When he died he left behind his body on the wood and ascended to the Good.

Justin's book *Baruch* contains all kinds of references to the Old and New Testaments and to Greek mythology. The serpentine body of Eden seems to be akin to an Egyptian notion of Isis.[30] Thus Justin commended Jesus to people from the Hellenistic world as the Redeemer who teaches people that their souls are destined to rise to the Father and to the Good. By comparison with other gnostic systems it is striking that here there is no break in the divine world; from the beginning Eloim and Eden are in ignorance about the Good. Only later does the male Eloim discover the way on high, while the female Eden is doomed to remain on earth. The question of the origin of evil on earth is thus answered by telling of the disappearance of Eloim, the God of the Old Testament. His disappearance unleashes doom on earth, while at the same time it makes the way free to the highest good God.

Justin incorporated the saying 'what no eye has seen, nor ear heard, nor the heart of man conceived' into the oath that he made his followers swear, to keep these mysteries secret. But Hippolytus got hold of a copy of the book *Baruch* and made this system known (in far more detail than I have described). He says that this is the worst heresy he has encountered.[31]

8. *Marcion*

Marcion was a shipowner from Sinope in Pontus, Asia Minor, where according to Epiphanius his father was a catholic bishop. Around the year 140 Marcion came to Rome, where (like Valentinus at that time) he became a member of the catholic community. However, in 144 he was excommunicated from this community for his heretical views. These views are known because a number of church fathers combated Marcion and the church which he founded. They often put him in a line with heretics like Simon the Magician, Menander, Valentinus and Basilides.[32] When Polycarp, the bishop of Smyrna, once met Marcion, he called him 'the first-born of Satan'.[33]

Marcion preached that there was an infinite distance between the righteous but also cruel God of the Old Testament and the unknown highest God of perfect love, the Father of Jesus. According to Irenaeus, Marcion learned this in Rome from the Simonian Cerdo, but it is also possible that Marcion had already developed his views in Sinope.[34] Marcion's verdict on the Creator who had created humankind body and soul, and from whom the law of Moses had come, was negative. In his view this Creator had not known that there was another God above him.[35] The affinity of these views to those of some gnostic teachers is manifest. However, one difference from most gnostics is that Marcion did not teach that the human being had a spiritual part of the highest God in him.[36] Still, this element does correspond with the teaching of Justin the Gnostic.

Thus although humankind was completely separated from the highest God, in his love he sent Jesus Christ to the earth. However, Jesus came in a phantom body, because the highest God had nothing to do with the material human body.[37] Jesus' task was to proclaim to human beings the grace of his unknown Father and to ransom them from the Creator by means of his death on the cross.[38] On his descent into hell he redeemed the unrighteous of the Old Testament like Cain, the inhabitants of Sodom, the Egyptians and other pagans. But Old Testament righteous like Abel, Enoch, Noah, the patriarchs and the prophets could not be redeemed by Jesus because they had attached themselves too much to the Creator.[39]

Marcion was strongly influenced by the letters of Paul. He drew a sharp distinction between the law and the gospel and he rejected the Old Testament as the authoritative book for the church.[40] He made a collection of ten abbreviated letters of Paul, from which he had removed all kinds of references to the Old Testament. The only Gospel that Marcion recognized was that of Luke, but he had also first removed Old Testament and Jewish elements from that. He expounded his views in a book called *Antitheses*.[41]

Because he wanted to exclude any collaboration with the Creator, he forbade his disciples to marry and prescribed sexual continence for married converts.[42] Despite the lack of natural growth through the birth of children, his church lasted for centuries.

It is not customary to reckon Marcion among the 'gnostics', although he is unmistakably akin to them and therefore the church fathers put him in line with them. Presumably Marcion derived from gnostic teachers the notion that the good Father of Jesus was one thing and the God of the Old Testament another. However, he did not outline any mythical system which explained in what way the human being has a nucleus which comes from the highest God. Nor does the element of recollection (or gnosis) of the higher divine world appear in Marcion. Instead, he wanted to base his teaching exclusively on Paul's view of Jesus, having first removed Old Testament elements from it. The result was an ascetic Christianity which was cut off from its Jewish roots.

9. Mani

Unlike the teachers discussed so far, Mani comes from the third century. He was born in 216 in Ctesiphon on the Tigris, in Babylonia. There he grew up in a group of Jewish-Christian 'baptists' who regularly performed ritual baptisms. However, on the instigation of his 'twin', i.e. his guardian angel or *alter ego,* Mani broke with these baptists. Presumably he then joined the Marcionites, but he did not stay with them either. Mani felt personally called to make known the true religion of the light, as an apostle of Jesus Christ. He probably regarded himself as the Paraclete, the holy Spirit who had been promised according to the Gospel of John;[43] in any case, his followers gave him this role. Mani made long journeys to proclaim his religion, as far as India. In contrast to the teachers already discussed, a large number of texts about him and partially from him have been preserved. These have been handed down not only by Mani's opponents but largely also by his followers, the Manichees.[44]

According to Mani, from the very beginning God the Father ruled over the realm of light, and alongside it there existed a realm of darkness and matter. But when the darkness wanted to attack the light and take it into itself, God the Father, with the help of the Mother of life, sent the first Man as a counter-attack. This mythical first Man was captured by the darkness, with the result that the darkness took into itself a being from the realm of light. As a result, elements of this light spread over the realm of darkness. In this way darkness was prevented from attacking the realm of light and wanting to take it entirely into itself.

Through the living Spirit and with the help of the Mother of life, the first Man was redeemed from the realm of darkness and returned to his fatherland. But elements of the light which had come from the soul of the first Man were left behind everywhere in the realm of darkness. The living Spirit and the Mother of life created the world from this realm of darkness and these elements of light. However, the powers of darkness created Adam and Eve, who were blind and deaf and had no sense of the light that was also in them. But the Redeemer, named Jesus the splendour of light, called Adam and revealed to him the knowledge about the light in him. Adam stands for the human being who recalls his origin from the light and so comes to the true insight. Because this knowledge is revealed through this Jesus, the Manichees know an intimate piety directed to Jesus.

The myth outlined by Mani was much more developed than the account of it here. All kinds of elements in it can be derived from Persian religion, but the influence of the apostle Paul and of Christian gnosticism can also be found in Mani's system. Mani's followers are to be divided into the 'elect' or 'perfect', who lived an unmarried and ascetic life, and 'hearers', who went less far in their observance of the precepts and might marry. With their gifts they supported the 'perfect', and thus at the same time profited from their piety. According to Mani, reincarnation usually awaits the souls of the hearers after earthly life, while the souls of the perfect will be redeemed at their deaths.

According to Mani the final goal of the world is for light and darkness again to be completely divided and for the darkness never again to be able to attack the light. This partly Christian and very dualistic gnosis had many adherents for centuries, from China to Western Europe. The fact that Mani provided his religion with a clear organization into two levels of followers doubtless contributed to this. This made it possible for people who wanted to commit themselves in a less radical way to find their place in it. Thus the later church father Augustine (354–430) lived as a Manichaean hearer for nine years, in his twenties.

11

Some gnostic and related texts

Of the many writings which have been found in Nag Hammadi I shall be discussing four here, three of which are called 'Gospel'. We do not know the real author of any of these writings, although two are attributed to the apostles Thomas and Philip respectively. Fifthly, I shall discuss 'The Hymn of the Pearl', which is included in the apocryphal Acts of Thomas.

1. The Gospel of Thomas

The discovery of the Coptic writing which bears the title 'The Gospel of Thomas' was spectacular because it contains a large number of sayings, parables and short dialogues in which Jesus speaks. It is in the second Nag Hammadi codex, where it follows one of the versions of the Secret Book of John. It is introduced as: 'These are the secret words which the living Jesus spoke and which Didymus Judas Thomas wrote down.' Although it was known that there had been a Gospel in the name of Thomas,[1] until the 1950s this writing had remained largely unknown. Certainly some Greek sayings of Jesus had already been found in Egypt, in a fragmentary state on papyrus, one fragment of which now proves to contain the beginning of this same 'Gospel of Thomas'.[2]

The writing is divided into 114 'words'.[3] To a notable degree these are related to the New Testament Gospels according to Matthew, Mark and Luke, and to a much lesser degree to that according to John. In the Gospel of Thomas, however, there are a large number of sayings which were previously unknown and which at least in nucleus could indeed come from Jesus.

It has always been a point of discussion how far the Gospel of Thomas can be called gnostic.[4] If we were to measure its gnostic character by the appearance of a highest God and a lower Creator, then it would be true that this distinction does not appear explicitly in these sayings. Far less can a developed myth like that in the Secret Book of John be found in this Gospel. But the distinction between two gods can possibly be inferred from this Gospel: the highest God is then called 'the Father' or 'the living Father' and the lower God of the Jews is called 'God'.[5] Another feature that can be called 'gnostic' is that here Jesus says to his disciples that they are from the kingdom and from the light,[6] which points to the preexistence of their souls in heaven. As in other apocryphal sources, here too Jesus speaks of the future male-female unity of the human being which was also in the beginning.[7] The emphasis on the secret knowledge about Jesus into which Thomas himself has been initiated,[8] the self-knowledge which is necessary to enter the kingdom of the Father,[9] may similarly be called gnostic. 'For whoever knows all but lacks (or does not know) himself lacks everything.'[10] Here there is a reference to the knowledge of one's own heavenly origin and destiny. Thus many sayings can be understood in a gnostic sense, and in my view this interpretation is also the correct one.[11] That the gnostic character of this collection is not equally evident everywhere accords with what is announced in the first two sayings. There the reader or hearer is urged to seek the meaning of these words in order to find it and so as not to have to taste death. Thus the true meaning is not given but remains concealed. The fact that it was in use among the Manichees[12] also argues in favour of the gnostic tenor of this Gospel.

Apart from the gnostic character, the dating of this Gospel is also a point of discussion. The question is whether the collector of these sayings knew and used the New Testament Gospels or whether he drew on a separate tradition. Some scholars go so far as to date this Gospel in the period between 50 and 70. In that case this collection would be older than the New Testament Gospels.[13] However, it is more probable that this collection, which indeed can contain very old traditions, was revised and supplemented in a gnostic direction in the second century. It is most probable that this Gospel was originally written in Greek and originated in Syria.[14]

2. *The Gospel of Philip*

In the second Nag Hammadi Codex, the 'Gospel of Philip' follows the Gospel of Thomas. This writing contains a collection of sayings, reflections on and interpretations of texts from the Old and New Testaments.[15] Apart from a number of quotations from the New Testament Gospels, Jesus is introduced only a few times in this collection as a speaker.[16] One saying (on p.73 of the codex) is in the name of the apostle Philip, and probably gave the Gospel its name. Here, too, it was known that a writing of this name existed before it was discovered in Nag Hammadi and that the Manichees used it. It is assumed that it was written around the year 200 in Greek, probably in Syria.[17]

In many passages there are allusions to a more developed mythology of the kind to be found among the Valentinians and in the Secret Book of John. Thus there is mention of Echamoth or Sophia and of Echmoth, the 'little Sophia'.[18] According to this Gospel (p.75 of the codex) the world came into being through a mistake or a transgression. The Creator wanted to make it imperishable and immortal, but he came to grief and did not achieve what he had hoped; it is said that neither the world nor the Creator are imperishable. Several times this lower Creator is called 'God'.[19] His angelic powers, the robbers or archons, are also mentioned.[20] There is often mention of the Father, who as the highest God is also the Father of Christ, the Son.[21] The writer mentions the healing and hidden work of the holy Spirit many times.[22] He makes a clear distinction between those who have gnosis and those who do not. He refers to his own group as 'Christians'.[23] He gives fine descriptions of their gnosis, which acquaints them with the truth and frees them from ignorance and evil.[24] The believers who still lack the true knowledge are called 'Hebrews' or also 'orphans'.[25] The term 'bridal chamber' is used repeatedly; this is a reference to the mystical union of the soul of the initiated Christians with their angels in heaven. Thus Christ as Redeemer has come to abolish the division between male and female in human beings, which arose in the beginning.[26] Another symbol for the mystical redemption is the resurrection of the dead, which already takes place during earthly life and is connected with baptism and anointing with oil.[27]

The Gospel of Philip presents a profound gnostic Christianity in which people were aware that the ultimate truth can be known only in symbols and images.[28] It regularly proves that these gnostics had a polemical attitude towards ordinary believers who were said to lack the essential knowledge.

3. The Gospel of Truth

The writing which is called the 'Gospel of Truth' appears in the first and twelfth Nag Hammadi codices.[29] Unlike the two 'Gospels' just discussed, it has no title. However it begins 'The gospel of truth is joy for those who have received from the Father of truth the grace of knowing him, through the power of the Word.' Now Irenaeus writes that the disciples of Valentinus had recently composed a work under the title 'Gospel of Truth'.[30] It is quite possible that here Irenaeus is referring to the writing found in Nag Hammadi which begins with these words; at any rate it has become customary to give it this title.

It has a different character from the collections of sayings discussed above, which are also called 'Gospels'. The Gospel of Truth is a meditative, mystical address about redemption from ignorance and about the riches of the knowledge of the truth. God the Father is called the Incomprehensible and the

Unthinkable. The All (the spiritual world) had come forth from him and was in him. Error is named as the figure who created matter and brought about fear and forgetfulness in the All (17). Jesus Christ is the Redeemer who has assumed a body and emerged as teacher. Thus he has made known the way to the Father and to the knowledge of truth (18–19). His death on the cross means life for many. His resurrection is described as the removal of the perishable rags (namely his body), after which he put on incorruption (20).

The holy Spirit is regarded as the bosom and tongue of the Father which binds believers with the Father (24; 26–27). This world is regarded as the place of deficiency, where envy and dispute reign and where the Father is unknown (24). Anyone who has received the knowledge of truth 'knows where he has come from and whither he shall go' and will also speak to others who seek the truth (22; 32; 41). The place in which those who have received 'knowledge' will have a part and to which they will go is called 'rest' and 'fullness' (*pleroma*) (34–35; 40–43).

Most of the reflections in this address will have sounded somewhat unusual in a catholic community, but perhaps would have been accepted there. However, the writing gives the impression that unorthodox views are not being developed explicitly (perhaps on purpose), as in the case of the Error which began to create matter. Thus it is also said that the Word of the Father cleanses the All and restores it to the Father and the Mother (24), without explaining who this Mother is.

It has been thought that this address was composed by Valentinus himself, but this view has been rejected – on good grounds – as being too speculative.[31] Irenaeus in fact attributed the writing with this name to the disciples of Valentinus, and said that they had composed it *recently*. Probably it was set down in writing around 150–170 in Rome. The original language was Greek.

4.The Treatise on the Resurrection

In the first Nag Hammadi codex, the Gospel of Truth is followed by the 'Treatise on the Resurrection'; this is a doctrinal letter by an anonymous author addressed to his pupil Rheginus. [32] Rheginus is exhorted not to doubt in the resurrection of the dead (47). To this end the author refers to the resurrection of Christ, which has swallowed up death. With reference to 'the apostle' (Paul) is is stated that we have suffered with Christ, risen with him and gone with him to heaven (45–46).[33] Thus the 'spiritual resurrection' has already taken place in this life, but there is also mention of a resurrection immediately after the death of the body. The believers will then assume 'flesh', but it is to be inferred from the letter that this has a different substance from the earthly body, and is like that of Moses and Elijah when they appeared to Jesus on the Mountain (47–48). The view of this author seems to be related to that of Paul, who in connection with the resurrection of the dead speaks of a 'spiritual body'.[34]

However, the author does not refer only to Paul but also to terms and notions which can be called gnostic. The believer already existed (clearly in heavenly pre-existence) before entering into a fleshly body in this world, and is destined to rise to eternity (*aion*) (47). It is characteristic that this world is called an illusion (*phantasia*) (48). Christ is called a seed of the truth. As Son of God he would overcome death and as Son of man he would bring about the return to fullness (*pleroma*) (44).

This letter is usually dated to the second half of the second century and is connected with the Valentinians.[35] This writing too was originally composed in Greek.

5. The Hymn of the Pearl

The apocryphal Acts of Thomas relate at length how the apostle Thomas preached the Christian faith in India. The Christianity which appears in it is very ascetic. The ideal is to live in sexual continence and thus to dedicate oneself wholly to Jesus as the true bridegroom. This form of Christianity occurred often in Syria. In fact these Acts were originally written in Syriac; they are dated to the third century.[36]

It is related that Thomas was imprisoned because of his activity. At this point a hymn has been inserted into one Syriac manuscript which Thomas is said to have sung at that time; this is known as the 'Hymn of the Pearl'.[37] This hymn is probably older than the Acts; it can be dated to the second or the beginning of the third century.[38]

In this hymn a king's son tells how his parents sent him to Egypt from their palace in the East to bring back a pearl which was guarded in the sea there by a serpent. He had to leave his glittering coat and his red toga at home, but if he returned with the pearl he would be clothed in them again. Then he would become heir in their kingdom with his brother, who was to remain behind in the palace. He took two guides with him, but they left him when he arrived in Egypt. In Egypt the prince entered an inn, where he felt a stranger amidst the other guests. However, there was one other person from the East, who kept him company. In order not to attract attention he dressed like the Egyptians. But because they observed that he was not one of them they gave him some of their food, which made him fall asleep. The prince forgot that he was a king's son and that he had come to get the pearl; he served the king of Egypt. However, the prince's parents got to know of this. They sent him a letter to awaken him from his sleep and to remind him that he was a king's son and that he had gone to Egypt to get the pearl. The letter took the form of an eagle, which flew to him and became all speech. On hearing its voice the prince woke up. He read the letter and remembered everything. In the name of his father, his brother and his mother he bewitched the serpent, seized the pearl, put off his unclean Egyptian clothes and returned, guided by the letter, to the light of his birth-place. His parents sent the glittering cloak and the toga to meet him. When he saw these, he saw that he had been separated from them. The cloak radiated knowledge and whispered to him that they fitted each other perfectly. The prince put on the cloak and the toga and was received into the palace, where he could appear before his father with the pearl.

It is clear that this fairy-tale hymn is meant as a parable and thus has a deeper meaning. All kinds of attempts have been made to interpret it; much has been written on the question whether this hymn can be called gnostic.[39]

Probably the prince who is sent to Egypt stands for the human soul which has fallen from heaven into the material world and there has forgotten its high origin and destiny. The cloak and the toga which he left behind in the palace then refer to the spirit and spiritual body with which the soul was originally united; the Egyptian clothes stand for the material body. As soon as the soul is awoken from its slumber by the letter in the form of an eagle,[40] becomes aware of its task and carries it out, it returns to its heavenly origin.

It is striking that the parents of the king's son deliberately send him from their palace to Egypt. This means that according to this hymn earthly existence is not so much the result of an unintentional fall from heaven, but that it has a purpose and a task for human beings. The acquisition of the pearl is then the symbol of this task. In the Gospel according to Matthew (13.45–46) and the Gospel of Thomas (76) there is a parable in which the pearl stands for the kingdom of God. However, the motif of the pearl in this hymn need not necessarily come from these Gospels and thus have the same meaning. The pearl can be explained as the essential thing in life, in other words, the essential knowledge.

The question whether this hymn may be called 'gnostic' is less interesting to the degree that the limits of what may be called gnostic are drawn less sharply. There is no compelling reason to explain the serpent which guards the pearl as the lower God of the world, but this is certainly possible. It is striking that the cloak is said to radiate knowledge (*gnosis* in the Greek translation). It is also important that the Acts of Thomas were used by the ('gnostic') Manichees, who perhaps also inserted this hymn into this book. But the Syrian church also accepted this work as it was and handed it down.[41]

Whether it is 'gnostic' or not, in any case Platonic motifs can be recognized in this hymn, like the pre-existence of the soul in heaven, its stay as a stranger on earth, recollection of its origin and return to heaven.[42] By its inclusion in the Acts of Thomas this hymn, which is not in itself explicitly Christian, is put in the mouth of the apostle Thomas. Thus it can be seen how the Syrian form of Christianity attested in these Acts was quite compatible with the Platonism expressed in this hymn.

Part IV   Christian faith and gnosis

12

The gnosis of some church fathers

In Chapter 8 it proved that the New Testament speaks quite unconcernedly about the *gnosis* of Christian faith, although there are also warnings against an autonomous gnosis. Moreover I referred there to some other writings from the end of the first and the beginning of the second centuries in which this use of the term gnosis is continued.[1] Afterwards, too, when the church was entangled in ever fiercer rivalry with 'heretical' gnosis, the church fathers use the term gnosis in their own way. Irenaeus is one example of this. On the basis of Paul's terminology, in the face of the so-called gnosis of the heretics he referred to the true gnosis of the one God which can be known in Jesus Christ crucified.[2] He then emphasized that our gnosis is always incomplete and that we have to leave speculative questions to God.[3]

In connection with the development of a distinctive form of gnosis the Alexandrian church fathers Clement and Origen deserve particular attention; after that I shall refer to Evagrius, who is in line with them. On the one hand Clement and Origen opposed the 'heretical' gnosis, but on the other they sometimes also seem to be related to it.

1. *Clement of Alexandria*

Clement reports that the Valentinians drew a distinction between their own gnosis and the faith of the church. Those who possessed gnosis would be redeemed through the special seed which was in them by nature; by contrast they regarded those who had only faith as 'simple'. Their own spiritual gnosis was far removed from this simple faith, which in their view was only 'psychic' (and thus lacked the Spirit).[4]

In the light of this Valentinian distinction it is striking that Clement also draws a distinction between gnosis and faith – but in a different way. He fully recognizes the simple faith that is based on Scripture, but he regards gnosis as the perfection of this faith.[5] Clement describes this gnosis in many ways. It includes the allegorical exposition of Scripture; in his view the Bible must often be interpreted spiritually, and not literally.[6] Jesus had handed down this knowledge to the apostles in an oral 'gnostic tradition'.[7] Clement also thinks that Greek schooling and the study of philosophy contribute to the acquisition of knowledge. Thus with the help of gnosis a believer can learn how the world came into being and what good and evil is; with this knowledge he can learn to investigate his faith critically and learn to give an account of it.[8] Clement also uses the term gnosis for the mystical knowledge that the soul acquires in the contemplation of God.[9] He thinks that when the souls want to rise to God after the death of the body, angels watch out for them and demand a toll of them. Gnosis and righteousness are the conditions for being admitted by these angels.[10]

In the previous chapters I have already remarked several times that Clement calls the believer who has acquired gnosis a 'gnostic'. With this terminology he seems to want to compete with the 'heretical' gnostics. He seems to want to say that the true gnosis and the true gnostics are to be found in the 'catholic church'.[11] Sometimes Clement's views and explanations of the Bible are related to those of the 'heretical' gnostics, but in general he distances himself from them and challenges them.[12] However, like other gnostics, Clement is strongly influenced by Middle Platonic philosophy. Yet he never goes so far as to attribute the creation of the world to a lower or inferior Creator; indeed he praises the good order in creation.[13] In Clement, the angels who watch out for the ascending souls to judge whether they may go further belong to the one God and not to a lower power. He also denies the

Platonic view that human souls already existed prior to their earthly life.[14]

Although Clement sometimes writes critically about simple faith, he maintains that it is indispensable for the gnostic as a foundation and cannot be detached from gnosis.[15] In addition, he also calls ordinary believers 'spiritual' if they have laid aside the fleshly desires and live in accordance with the commandment to love.[16] Clement occupied a remarkable position in his time, given that he began to stand in the field of tension between the 'catholic church' and 'heretical' gnosis.

2. Origen

Origen writes many times about the gnosis of Christian faith, as was customary in the church of the time. But in a similar way to Clement he too draws a distinction between the gnosis of the advanced or 'perfect' and the belief of the simple Christians. According to Origen, these simple Christians concentrated their faith on the man Jesus Christ who was crucified. But without denying this faith, he thinks that what really matters is the knowledge of Jesus Christ who is spiritually present as God's Word and Wisdom. Origen understands the apostle Paul as having had a message on two levels, for the simple and for the advanced.[17]

Unlike Clement, then, Origen does not use the term 'gnostic' for advanced, spiritual Christians.[18] He probably thought that this name could be misunderstood as relating to the heretical gnostics.[19] He constantly fought against these gnostics. Origen assented to the 'apostolic preaching' and despite his criticism of some bishops always remained loyal to the church.[20] Thus he confessed with the church of the apostles that there is one God who has created everything and is God of the Old and New Testament. Jesus Christ is born of God the Father from eternity and although he was God, became man. He truly suffered and truly died and rose from the dead. However, Origen thought that the church's confession did not give an answer to various questions that could be raised by philosophy. Indeed he felt free to seek answers to these questions, and in so doing made use of Platonic categories. Thus he stated that the church's preaching was not clear about the origin of the soul and the origin of the devil and his angels. It was also unclear what there was before this world was created, and what there will be after this world.[21]

Origen tried to give answers to these questions. However, he presented his answers as suppositions and not as a doctrine which could not be doubted. Thus he supposed that God's creation was originally only spiritual and not material. God created 'beings endowed with reason' who were equal in rank to one another. Through their mind (*nous*) these creatures have a free will. However, they misused this will to rebel against God. The consequence of this was a dramatic fall in which each creature fell deeper, depending on the degree to which it had sinned against God. This gave rise to a hierarchy based on this primal fall. In order to catch the falling creatures God created a material world. The angels in heaven continued to stand above; they had rejected God the least. The devil and his angels, who instigated the rebellion against God, are of quite a different order. God created the heavenly bodies of the planets for a particular category of fallen creatures. For another category he created human bodies on earth to catch their fallen mind (*nous*) in them; this *nous*, however, was cooled down (*psychesthai*) to become soul (*psyche*). Only the soul which was destined for Christ on earth had not taken part in this rebellion.[22]

Human beings can recollect their former life with God.[23] If they want to return to God again after this life, they are looked out for by angels who demand a toll of them; the 'prince of this world', the devil, is one of these 'toll-keepers'.[24] The purpose of God's material creation is, in Origen's view, to return to the beginning again. At the end everything will be restored to its spiritual state. The resurrection of the dead will then take place in 'spiritual bodies'.[25] Origen did keep open the possibility that after this restoration there might be another fall into matter. The creatures would keep their free will and could thus rebel against God again, after which another material creation would be necessary. That could give rise to a cycle of worlds, but according to Origen this would not go on endlessly; God's love would finally overcome the tendency to rebellion and defection.[26]

Like Clement, Origen thinks that the Bible has to be interpreted allegorically.[27] This starting point gave him the possibility of interpreting all kinds of texts from the Old and New Testaments spiritually, with reference to his own views. Allegorical interpretation contributed to the preservation in the church of the Old Testament, which was sometimes felt to be difficult.

It is evident from this survey of some of Origen's views that he interpreted Christian faith in a way which sometimes suggests the gnostics.[28] However, it is important that he attributes the creation of this world to the one God and not to a lower Creator. According to Origen, the fact that human beings live on this earth is a result of the choice which the soul once made when it joined in the rebellion against God (as *nous*). In his view, the soul is thus itself responsible for its existence in the earthly body. He thought that the fact that the fallen soul has found its way into a body is a gracious disposition of God, seeing that in this body it can learn to return to God again through Christ.[29] Thus Origen opposes the view that he encountered in gnostics, namely that by nature they were already spiritual and elect. However, Origen's view that the purpose of human beings is once again to be completely spiritual and to leave the material body behind them is akin to the gnostics.

Many simple believers could not or would not follow Origen's profound arguments – his *gnosis*. Despite the difficulties which this repudiation had caused Origen, he always reckoned the simple to be part of the church and defended them against the mockery of outsiders.[30] In this respect Origen thus differs from the gnostics, who were inclined to look down on the catholic believers, who were said to have no gnosis. Thus like Clement, Origen occupied a middle position between the church and the gnostics – although he reckoned himself completely part of the church.

3. *Evagrius of Pontus*

The designation of the purpose of Christian life as gnosis also continued in the catholic church of the fourth century. One example of this can be found in Evagrius of Pontus. He lived in the second half of the fourth century and from 383 until his death in 399 was a monk in the Egyptian desert. He must have studied the works of Origen thoroughly, since many of Origen's ideas recur in him. Unlike Origen, Evagrius had no problem in using the term 'gnostic'; here we can see the influence of Clement.

Evagrius thinks that a monk who strives for gnosis must first overcome the impulses and passions of his sinful 'old man'. He calls this phase, in which one can learn to oppose the evil spirits which summon up all kinds of bad thoughts and desires, *praktike*. He described this 'practice' in a hundred sayings.[31] Some one who has become a 'practic' has learned to pray and has made his own the commandment to love. After that the way is free for him to become a 'gnostic'. In various collections of sayings Evagrius describes what the gnosis needed for this involves. His sayings have been preserved partly in Greek and more extensively in two Syriac translations. Of these two Syriac translations, one has been expurgated according to orthodox standards; the other gives Evagrius' original thoughts better.[32]

The purpose of Evagrius' gnosis is for the monk to be drawn to the vision of the triune God during and after earthly life.[33] In a sometimes very cryptic way he speaks of the fall of spiritual creatures before the world, as Origen had supposed it.[34] Not only Origen's view of the spiritual resurrection of the dead[35] but also allusions to a possible recurrence of the fall into matter can be found in Evagrius.[36] In these sayings many allegorical explanations of biblical texts can be found. In all this mystical and speculative knowledge, Evagrius does not forget that the gnostic needs above all else to be ready to do good.[37]

Presumably Evagrius' use of the terms gnosis and gnostic has a polemical point, as was also the case with Clement. In the fourth century, too, there were 'heretical' gnostics in Egypt, as is evident from the Coptic manuscripts of Nag Hammadi which were made at this time. Indeed Evagrius regularly attacks 'so-called' or 'false' gnosis, but without going more deeply into its content.[38]

4. The early church and its gnostic tradition

It is evident from this discussion of Clement, Origen and Evagrius that the catholic church of the first centuries had its own gnostic tradition. This gnosis, which was meant only for advanced Christians, eventually had to lead to the mystical contemplation of God, during life in the earthly body and afterwards. Moreover this gnosis contained a theory about the origin and disappearance of the material world, in which everything would be completely spiritual.

However, the speculative character of this knowledge for initiates caused great suspicion in the catholic church. From the end of the fourth century on, a vigorous dispute flared up over this heritage, when it proved that many monks were orientated on it.[39] During or shortly before the Council of Constantinople in 553 their viewpoints – which at that time were especially attributed to Origen – were rejected and condemned.[40] The then Roman emperor, Justinian, was an important motive force behind this condemnation. This was because he wanted to rid his empire of the old pagan influences. For this reason, in 529, two years after his accession as emperor, he had closed the neo-Platonic philosophical school in Athens. It is evident from a letter which he wrote to Patriarch Menas of Constantinople that he saw Origen as a mouthpiece for Greek mythology and Plato.[41] Thus the condemnation of Origen and Origenistic monks was a late attempt to call a halt to this form of the Hellenizing of Christianity.

13

Gnosis assessed

In the first centuries of our era the church fathers rejected and disputed the various trends of 'heretical' gnosis. It would require a separate study to indicate in detail what their arguments were; such a study would also bring to light all kinds of other aspects of gnosis than those which I have discussed so far.[1] That would take us too far here. So instead of offering a detailed study of the objections to gnosis put forward by the early church, in this chapter I shall offer an overall survey in which I shall distinguish some main lines.

Thus far I have tried to discuss the material as objectively and historically as possible. Thus in the provisional summary in Chapter 9 gnosis was described as neutrally as possible as 'a form of Hellenized Christianity'. However, there is no mistaking the fact that gnosticism not only provoked reactions then but also does so in our times, both of acceptance and rejection. Some think that the gnostics were wrongly branded heretics by the church; others agree in principle with the decisions that were taken in the early church about the Christian faith. Moreover it is also possible to stand in between and recognize oneself both in some gnostic and also in particular orthodox Christian standpoints.

So in this last chapter, by means of the church fathers I want to arrive at an evaluation of some arguments for and against ancient gnosticism.

1. Is not God the Father at the same time the Creator?

There are all kinds of differences between the church fathers, as there are between the various gnostic tendencies. Nevertheless they all agree in their fundamental objection to the gnostic distinction between a higher good God the Father and a lower God the Creator and his creator angels. Irenaeus is never tired of bearing witness that there is one God who embraces all things and who made all things, visible and invisible, through his Word. According to Irenaeus this means that with the Word – Jesus Christ – as the one through whom he created the world, God has also ensured the redemption of human beings in this creation.[2] Tertullian, Hippolytus, Clement and Origen also reject the gnostic view that there is a separate Creator who stands far below the true highest God in rank. This means that for the church fathers the God of the Old Testament is the same as the God of the New Testament. In short, according to them there is one God who has made himself known in the creation, in Abraham, Moses and the prophets and in Jesus Christ. The church fathers also were able to connect even the difficult parts of the Old Testament with God the Father of Jesus Christ.[3]

In Chapter 9.4 I already indicated that the choice made by many gnostics, namely to distinguish the God of the Old Testament from the Father of Jesus Christ, is in some senses understandable. From the creation story onwards, many parts of the Old Testament give the impression that the Lord God is all too human and is thus not sufficiently exalted. It seems possible to characterize him in terms of meaningless commandments, cruelties that are difficult to justify, capriciousness and narrow-minded arrogance. At most it could still be said of this God that he is righteous, but – in this view – he is in no way good. It proved possible to explain the solution which many gnostics chose, namely to degrade the Old Testament to a book which predominantly speaks of a lower God, in terms of Platonism.

It goes without saying that the consequences of this split in

God are far-reaching. If the God who sends the Redeemer from his high heaven has not created the world, then he is a stranger on this earth. In that case the earth is not his domain. Then it makes no sense to say that 'our help is in the name of the Lord who has made heaven and earth' (Ps. 124.8). This world, including the planets, would then be in the grip of lower powers whose influence one had to be careful to escape. The efforts of the highest God with the earth then seem to go no further than the redemption of the divine nucleus in those human beings who have been brought to the true knowledge. The human body is said to have been created by the lower God or his angels. The question is what more life on earth is than a quest of the soul for the high heavenly world.

A second consequence of the gnostic splitting up of God is that belief in the concrete resurrection from the dead falls away. Gnostics often identified the resurrection of the dead with the acquisition of true gnosis during life on earth. After the death of the body the soul of the gnostic, possibly risen in a spiritual body, might return to the heavenly world of the highest God. By contrast, most church fathers drew from the belief that redemption comes from God the Creator the conclusion that God will restore the whole person. Thus the human being will one day be recreated soul and body. This 'resurrection of the flesh' is mentioned in the so-called 'Roman Creed' (the 'Apostles' Creed').[4] In line with this expectation was the view that life in this earthly body is also important and is willed by God. However, in their view of the resurrection, Clement and Origen stood closer to the gnostics, as they expected a spiritual resurrection, for which they referred back to Paul.[5]

A third consequence of the gnostic division between the God of the Old Testament and the Father of Jesus Christ has still to be mentioned. If the church had gone along with it, then the bond with the people of Israel would have been cut more than ever. The God of the Jewish people would then have been different from the Father by whom Jesus Christ knew he had been sent. Jesus would then not stand in the line of the Old Testament prophets, but would have proclaimed a completely new, heavenly message.

I think it a very good thing that the church fathers preserved the Old Testament as holy Scripture for the church. In so doing they made it clear that the Christian faith stems from God who has created life on earth and who has started on a history with humankind from the beginning. The view that this God willed life on earth and that he wanted to give it his blessing bears witness to trust and hope. This faith is opposed to the view that life in this world is to be reduced to a tragic and deeply meaningless event in the heavenly world. By starting from the Old Testament, Christian faith opposes the feeling that gnosticism causes, namely that life on earth is profoundly meaningless or serves only a heavenly purpose.

As for the gnostic longing of the soul to return above, it is true that the longing for heaven or – as it is called – the here-after, also has a legitimate place in Christian faith.[6] But the Christian expectation goes further. We can read in the New Testament (in a quotation from the Old Testament): 'in accordance with his (God's) promises we await a new heaven and a new earth in which righteousness shall dwell'.[7] I grant that this is an unimaginable promise – as unimaginable as the expectation of the resurrection of the dead. But I see good reasons for not dropping this perspective from the substance of Christian faith, as gnostics in fact did. I would not want to exchange the belief in God who spans the centuries for a personal mysticism which is only about the salvation of my soul and the souls of those who are like-minded to me. That is not to say anything against mysticism, but it is to oppose a gnostic narrowing of the Christian faith. The prospect of righteousness ruling on earth is closely connected with the call to live in this life in accordance with the righteousness that is to come. We can see an example of this in the whole of the 'second letter of Peter' from which I quoted the text about the new heaven and the new earth. The value of the Old Testament for the Christian church is that it reminds it of earthly justice and can protect it from a one-sided spiritualization.

Here it must be pointed out that the church fathers did not keep the Old Testament with the deliberate purpose of guarding the Christian faith against spiritualization. By means of allegorical interpretation they often spiritualized the Old Testament in a far-reaching way – but not totally. Far less did they revere the Old Testament with the purpose of keeping alive the bond with the Jewish people. In the first centuries a great gulf developed between Jews and Christians, even with the retention of the Old Testament. All too often the Christian church did not heed the appeal of the apostle Paul not to be arrogant and not to think that it knew better than the Jews (Rom. 11.20–25). But Paul's reflections on Israel (in Rom. 9–11) would become quite incomprehensible and fall victim to spiritualization all the more if the Old Testament were attributed to another God. The sense that Jews and Christians start from the same God would then have been completely lost.

In the above paragraphs I have presented some objections to the view which many gnostics had developed about the Old Testament and the God of Israel. However, I recall that in a writing like the Exegesis on the Soul, the Old Testament is quoted as an authoritative book and is applied to the redemption of the seeker. If we want to call this sermon gnostic, then this appeal to the Lord God of the Old Testament also seems to be possible among gnostics.[8]

I end these reflections with another comment which perhaps to some degree agrees with the old gnostics. In our time more than then there is room for the insight that both the Old and the New Testament contains human witnesses and views not all of which have an equal weight. It is now often accepted that offensive passages can be read as ancient texts which are remote from us and do not necessarily have authority for faith in this time. A distinction is made between the nucleus of the Bible and what lies around it: this means that one text has more authority than another. We have come to see the different genres in the Bible, each of which must be interpreted in its own way. Thus the hymnic and mythical creation stories must not be regarded as factual historiography.

In a similar but in my view far too incisive way this introduction of a distinction also occurs among the gnostics; one may think, e.g. of Ptolemaeus' 'Letter to Flora' (pp. 131f.). In a sense someone like Ptolemaeus is to be regarded as a distant forerunner of modern biblical exegesis.

2. Did Jesus Christ have a gnostic message?

In so far as gnostics thought that Jesus had not been authentically human but was only seemingly clothed with a human body, this provoked the criticism of the church fathers. As appears from a large number of witnesses, the gnostic view was held that the death and resurrection of Jesus Christ were also semblance; this made it impossible to attribute a redemptive value to them. In addition there were also gnostics who did attach importance to Christ's death and resurrection, as is evident from Theodotus, the Gospel of Truth and the Treatise on the Resurrection.[9] However, their interpretation of the cross and resurrection was in a framework which deviated from the catholic creed.

In the face of the docetism of the gnostics Irenaeus appeals to a large number of texts in the New Testament which attest that Jesus Christ, the Son of God, truly became man. His key witness is John 1.14, 'the Word became flesh'. Irenaeus explains that through Christ's death and resurrection human beings alienated from God are adopted again by God. He sees Christ as the second Adam who makes good the transgression of the first Adam. For Irenaeus the bodily resurrection of Christ is the pledge of the bodily resurrection which Christians may expect.[10] Tertullian agrees. He sees a close connection between Christ's true incarnation, death and resurrection on the one hand and on the other the redemption of human beings, soul and body, and their fleshly resurrection from the dead.[11] Nor does Hippolytus differ.[12]

Origen too defends the church's confession of the true incarnation, crucifixion and bodily resurrection of Christ.[13] However, he recognizes that Christ's resurrection body was different from the body that he had before his death.[14] By contrast, Clement is sometimes unclear as to whether Jesus had an ordinary human body; thus he thinks that while Jesus ate, his body did not need the food: Jesus had eaten in order to avoid people thinking that he had only apparently appeared as man![15] Nevertheless Clement reports that Christ died and rose as an atonement for us and the whole world, for the healing of our body and soul.[16]

It would take us too far to go in more depth here into the views that these church fathers had about redemption by the death and resurrection of Jesus Christ. However, I want to make one more remark on this: the later Protestant concentration of Christian faith on the death of Jesus as an atonement for our sins cannot be found in that form in the church fathers. Generally speaking they attached just as much importance to the incarnation and resurrection and glorification of the Son of God. As a matter of course they also saw Jesus Christ as the teacher sent by God – the God of the Old Testament.

Although, as I have said, gnostics sometimes also attached a redemptive significance to the death and resurrection of Jesus, for them Jesus was above all the divine emissary. Thus in the Gospel of Thomas Jesus appears as a wisdom teacher of secret words. In the Secret Book of John, after his resurrection Christ gives insight to John into the mysteries relating to the Father, the Mother, the Son and all the other powers. According to Cerinthus, Christ proclaimed the unknown Father. According to Justin the Gnostic, Jesus made known to human beings the (lower) Father and the Good. Usually Jesus is regarded in the gnostic writings as a messenger of the highest God and not of the lower Old Testament God.

In our day there is a special interest in Jesus as a teacher of the gnosis which cannot be found in the New Testament. For those who find it difficult to know what to make of the traditional Christian view of Jesus it can be a revelation that other words and stories of Jesus have been handed down. Once again I would mention the Gospel of Thomas, in which a number of sayings are attributed to Jesus which were previously unknown. In my discussion of the Gospel I observed that it is certainly possible that a number of these sayings indeed go back to Jesus.

However, the gnostic writings provoke the following questions. Is the picture of Jesus as a teacher of a special gnosis historically correct? Are fundamental elements of Jesus' teaching missing from the New Testament Gospels? Were the authors of the New Testament writings wrong in believing that the death and resurrection of Jesus brought redemption to human beings? Was Jesus not really rather a gnostic wisdom teacher? In short, the question is: was Jesus a gnostic?

My answer to these questions falls into three points. First, it seems clear to me – and to those who feel akin to ancient gnosticism – that Jesus was a man of flesh and blood. That gnostics doubted whether he was truly human derives from their Platonism (for this see Chapter 9.3). According to Platonism the highest God does not directly involve himself with matter. According to gnosis, which was related to this, Jesus could therefore only be the spiritual emissary of the highest God by adapting himself to humankind and clothing himself in a human body. He was a kind of angel who appeared in a body; however, this body was not essential. It seems to me that, historically speaking, the witness of the New Testament and the church fathers that Jesus was truly human carries more conviction. Here it says a great deal that early Christianity connected the man Jesus closely with God. That means that in this view God can become fully involved in human life and has no reason whatsoever for keeping his distance from a bodily existence.

This brings me to the second point. For gnostics, Jesus is the emissary of the highest God, who teaches true insight into the origin and destiny of human life. Now the gnostic emphasis on Jesus as a teacher corresponds with the New Testament

Gospels. These bear manifold witness to Jesus' teaching, both in public and in a smaller circle, both during his earthly life and after his resurrection. In the Gospel of John Jesus speaks of his heavenly origin and destiny in a way which sometimes even suggests gnosticism. However, a by no means negligible difference from the gnostic texts is that according to the New Testament and the church fathers Jesus is sent by the God of the Old Testament. In this view Jesus unambiguously stood in the line of Moses and the prophets. It seems to me indisputable that Jesus also saw himself in this way. So it is historically incorrect to regard Jesus as an emissary of an unknown God who far transcended the God of the Old Testament. This supposition was alien to Jesus. Gnostics introduced the Platonic distinction between the highest God and a lower Creator and Lawgiver into Christian faith; the church fathers rightly rejected it – understandable though it sometimes is.

It follows from this that revelations like those in the Secret Book of John cannot come from Jesus Christ – either from the earthly Jesus or from Christ after his resurrection. All kinds of gnostic ideas like those of disobedient Sophia and her tragic fruit Yaldabaoth and his angelic powers which keep watch on the planets do not offer any original Christian gnosis. It is very improbable that Jesus handed down a secret gnosis to his disciples apart from his public teaching; in any case I think that we can rule out the possibility that such teaching for initiates which was to be kept secret has now come to light in the books of Nag Hammadi. Moreover Jesus uttered an eloquent saying in the Gospel of John:

> I have spoken openly to the world; I have always taught in synagogues and in the temple, where all Jews come together; I have said nothing secretly.[17]

It does not conflict with this that according to Mark 4.11 and 4.34 Jesus explained the mystery of the kingdom of God to his disciples separately: this teaching is described in the New Testament Gospels.

The third point that I want to go into in connection with the gnostic view of Jesus concerns his crucifixion and resurrection. Taking up the first point, it seems to me indubitable that the man Jesus was really crucified. Any docetism that implies that Jesus or Christ was not really crucified but that he withdrew from his body beforehand seems to me to be unfounded. This docetism is rather to be explained from Platonism; for this see the first point.

As I explained earlier, according to the New Testament writings the death and resurrection of Jesus were for the redemption of humankind, in the sense of the forgiveness of sins and reconciliation with God. The church fathers maintained this redemptive significance of Jesus' death and resurrection in all kinds of variations. However, the apostle Paul attests that the proclamation of a crucified Christ also evoked repudiation and caused offence.[18] The gnostics, who interpreted the death of Jesus or Christ as Redeemer in a docetic way or passed over it, bear witness to this offence.

If Christ is viewed above all as a spiritual Redeemer who comes as a teacher of gnosis on earth and rises again on high, this also influences the view of his resurrection. While Jesus is then regarded as 'the living one',[19] in essence – in this view – he has never really died. That Jesus is the living one may be affirmed. However, in so far as this implies that his suffering, death and resurrection are given a subordinate role or are denied, this is far removed from the original Christian witness, which runs: 'Christ died for our sins according to the Scriptures, and was buried, and rose on the third day, according to the Scriptures.'[20]

My answers to the questions raised above about the possible 'gnostic' content of Jesus' person and teaching are thus all negative ones. This does not alter the fact that a fascination with the gnostic interpretation of Jesus is very understandable. Historically speaking, however, what we have here is a later Hellenistic development. Of course we can also see in the New Testament and in the church fathers that the early Christian views of Jesus underwent development. It would take us too far now to go more closely into this than we have done so far in some previous chapters (8.2; 12). I now have to conclude that the gnostic interpretation of the person and teaching of Jesus cannot lay claim to greater historical reliability and authenticity.

3. Was gnosticism elitist?

In Chapter 9.6 I said that the generalization that gnostic knowledge was reserved for an elite is not true. Gnostics were ready to share their special gnosis with others or saw this as their task. Nor did they always think that they alone had a share in redemption. The Secret Book of John appears to offer the prospect that all souls will be redeemed apart from those of the apostates. Gnostic Christians did not segregate themselves by definition. They did not initially always have a separate organization but also formed part of the 'catholic' communities. Initially the dividing line between 'gnostic' and 'catholic' Christianity was not always a sharp one.

However, the church fathers did draw this dividing line and accused heretical gnostics of wrongly regarding themselves as 'pneumatics' ('spiritual Christians'). Irenaeus, Tertullian, Hippolytus, Clement and Origen agreed here. In my discussion of the Valentinians Ptolemaeus and Theodotus it also emerged that they called other believers 'psychics', because they had no part in the Spirit. A third category of people was simply 'earthy'. According to gnostic insight this tripartite division of human beings was foreordained.[21]

Of course the church fathers could not (or did not want to) personally feel this gnostic sense of being chosen and preordained to the true knowledge of spiritual redemption. Therefore they perhaps exaggerated this aspect of gnosis in their accounts. But that does not alter the fact that they were disturbed at the gnostic sense of superiority which disqualified not only the simple believers but also catholic Christians generally. For even if gnostics wanted to show toleration for the psychics who lacked the true spiritual insight and thus

also the Spirit, they began from a gulf in knowledge and spiritual level.[22]

We could see from the discussion of Clement and Origen
that they made a similar distinction between simple believers
and advanced Christians. Only these advanced, 'gnostic' or
'perfect' Christians were said to have insight into the allegorical interpretation of the Bible and to be in a position to
express the faith in philosophical terms. However, Clement
and Origen never suggest that the simple believers would have
no part in the holy Spirit. They recognize that these simple
people too belong to the community of the apostolic church
which throughout this book I have called 'catholic'. Tertullian
was inclined to look down on the simple believers,[23] but when
he showed signs of this he had already left the catholic church
and joined the Montanists. By contrast, when Irenaeus speaks
of the 'perfect' who have the Spirit in themselves and live by
it, he is referring to all those who form part of the church of
the apostles.[24] According to Irenaeus this church is spread
over the whole world, though it stems from the one faith of
the apostolic tradition. He will have nothing of a superior
group within this church.[25]

It is possible that a number of gnostics did not intend to
stand out by their special insight and thus cause offence to
catholic Christians and their leaders. Nevertheless, this is the
effect that their rise had. The objection to the gnostics thus
related on the one hand to the content of their speculative
development of Christian faith, and on the other hand to the
attitude that they radiated, as if they knew better. Perhaps
gnostic knowledge was not always meant to be elitist, but that
is how it came over. (It is relevant that the philosopher
Plotinus also found that gnostics in his audience believed that
they knew better, as they thought that Plato had not searched
deep enough and it seemed as if they had fathomed out precisely how everything was.[26])

Over against these gnostics stood the church, which at that
time was called 'apostolic' and 'catholic'. 'Catholic' means
'universal' and was initially used to denote the world-wide

church and thus to distinguish it from a local church.[27] However, this term also has another meaning. 'Catholic' as a name for the Christian church also means that salvation is available for all believers and not simply for a particular group which has been initiated into a special gnosis.[28] This 'catholic' or 'universal Christian church' is like the unruly masses who stream round Jesus in the New Testament Gospels. It consists of a great crowd of disciples in the faith who are called 'Christians' for the first time in Antioch, and it consists of the simple in Corinth.[29] There is room in this church for both the simple and those with knowledge, preferably without anyone referring to a supposed sense of superior insight.

Bibliography

(Only some of the editions and translations of ancient texts used in this book have been included in this bibliography)

Achelis, H., *Hippolyt's kleinere exegetische and homiletische Schriften*, GCS 1, 2, Leipzig 1897

Aland, B., 'Gnosis and Kirchenväter', in B. Aland (ed.), *Gnosis. Festschrift für H. Jonas*, Göttingen 1978, 158–215

—, 'Marcion. Versuch einer neuen Interpretation', *Zeitschrift für Theologie und Kirche* 70, 1973, 420–47

Arai, S., 'Simonianische Gnosis und die *Exegese über die Seele*', in M. Krause (ed.), *Gnosis and Gnosticism. Papers read at the Seventh International Conference on Patristic Studies*, Leiden 1977, 185–203

Baarda, T., *Early Transmission of Words of Jesus*, Amsterdam 1983

—, *Essays on the Diatessaron*, Kampen 1994

Baltes, M., 'Numenios von Apamea und der platonische Timaios', *Vigiliae Christianae* 29, 1975, 241–70

Bammel, C. P, *Tradition and Exegesis in Early Christian Writers*, Aldershot 1995

Barker, M., *The Great Angel. A Study of Israel's Second God*, London 1992

Betz, H. D., 'Ein seltsames mysterientheologisches System bei Plurarch', in J. Bergman et al. (eds), *Ex orbe religionum. Studia Geo Widengren oblata*, Leiden 1972, 347–54

Beyer, B., 'Das syrische Perlenlied. Ein Erlösungsmythos als Märchengedicht', *Zeitschrift der Deutschen Morgenländischen Gesellschaft* 140, 1990, 234–59

Beyschlag, K., *Simon Magus und die simonianische Gnosis*, Tübingen 1974

Bianchi, U. (ed.), *Le origini dello gnosticismo. Colloquio di Messina 13–18 aprile 1966*, Leiden 1967

Bienert, W. A., *Dogmengeschichte*, Stuttgart, Berlin and Cologne 1997

Böhlig, A. et al., *Die Gnosis III. Der Manichäismus*, Zurich and Munich 1980

Bos, A. P., 'Cosmic and Meta-cosmic Theology in Greek Philosophy and Gnosticism', in W. E. Helleman (ed.), *Hellenization Revisited. Shaping a Christian Response within the Greco-Roman World*, Lanham, MA 1994, 1–21

Boulluec, A. le, *La notion d'hérésie dans la littérature grecque IIe–IIIe siècles*, I-II, Paris 1985

—, and Sandevoir, P., *La Bible d'Alexandrie 2: L'Exode*, Paris 1989

Boyancé, P., 'Dieu cosmique et dualisme. Les archontes et Platon', in U. Bianchi (ed.), *Le origini dello gnosticismo*, Leiden 1967, 340–56

Broek, R. van den, *Studies in Gnosticism and Alexandrian Christianity*, Leiden 1996

Brown, P., *The Body and Society. Men, Women and Sexual Renunciation in Early Christianity*, New York 1988 and London 1989

Bultmann, R., *'ginosko'*, *Theological Dictionary of the New Testament* I, Grand Rapids 1964, 689–719

Bunge, J. G., 'Origenismus – Gnostizismus. Zum geistesgeschichtlichen Standort des Evagrios Pontikos', *Vigiliae Christianae* 40, 1986, 24–54

Cadiou, R., *Commentaires inédits des Psaumes. Étude sur les textes d'Origène contenus dans le manuscrit Vindobonensis 8*, Paris 1936

Clark, E. A., *The Origenist Controversy. The Cultural Construction of an Early Christian Debate*, Princeton 1992

Colson, F. H., and Whittaker, G. H., *Philo in Ten Volumes (and Two Supplementary Volumes)*, Loeb Classical Library, London and Cambridge, Mass., 1929–1953

Desjardins, M., 'Judaism and Gnosticism', in W. E. Helleman (ed.), *Hellenization Revisited. Shaping a Christian Response within the Greco-Roman World*, Lanham, MA 1994, 309–21

Dodd, C. H., *The Bible and the Greeks*, London ³1964

Dörrie, H., 'Gnostische Spuren bei Plutarch', in R. van den Broek and M. J. Vermaseren (eds), *Studies in Gnosticism and Hellenistic Religions. Presented to G. Quispel*, Leiden 1981, 92–116

Edwards, M. J., 'The *Epistle to Rheginus*: Valentinianism in the Fourth Century', *Novum Testamentum* 37, 1995, 76–91

Fallon, F. T., and Cameron, R., 'The Gospel of Thomas: A Forschungsbericht and an Analysis', in W. Haase and H. Temporini (eds), *Aufstieg und Niedergang der Römischen Welt* II, 25, 6, Berlin and New York 1988, 4195–251.

Festugière, A. J., *La révélation d'Hermès Trismégiste III: Les doctrines de l'âme, IV: Le dieu inconnu et la gnose*, Paris ²1983

Filoramo, G., *A History of Gnosticism*, Oxford 1990

Fossum, J. E., *The Name of God and the Angel of the Lord*, Utrecht 1982

Franzmann, M., *Jesus in the Nag Hammadi Writings*, Edinburgh 1996

Görgemanns, H., and Karpp, H., *Origenes. Vier Bücher von den Prinzipien*, Darmstadt 1976

Gregg, J. A. F., 'The Commentary of Origen upon the Epistle to the Ephesians', II, *Journal of Theological Studies* 3, 1902, 398–420

Gruenwald, I., *From Apocalypticism to Gnosticism*, Frankfurt am Main 1988

Guillaumont, A., *Les 'Kephalaia Gnostica' d'Évagre le Pontique et l'histoire de l'origénisme chez les Grecs et chez les Syriens*, Paris 1962

—, *Les six centuries des 'Kephalaia Gnostica' d'Évagre le Pontique*, Paris 1958, Turnhout ²1985

—, A. and C., *Évagre le Pontique. Traité pratique ou le moine* II, Paris 1971

—, *Évagre le Pontique. Le Gnostique ou à celui qui est devenu digne de la science*, Paris 1989

Hällström, G. af, *Fides Simpliciorum according to Origen of Alexandria*, Helsinki 1984

Harnack, A. von, *Lehrbuch der Dogmengeschichte* I, Tübingen ⁵1931

—, *Marcion. Das Evangelium vom fremden Gott*, Leipzig ²1923, Darmstadt 1985

Helderman, J., 'Das Evangelium Veritatis in der neueren Forschung', in: W. Haase and H. Temporini (eds), *Aufstieg und Niedergang der Römischen Welt* II, 25, 6, Berlin and New York 1988, 4054–106

Hering, J., *Étude sur la doctrine de la chute et de la préexistence des âmes chez Clément d'Alexandrie*, Paris 1923

Heyer, C. J. den, *Jesus Matters. 150 Years of Research*, London and Valley Forge 1996
Holl, K., *Epiphanius. Ancoratus und Panarion*, GCS 25, 31, Leipzig 1915, 1922

Jonas, H., *Gnosis und Spätantiker Geist* II, ed. K. Rudolph, Göttingen 1993
—, *The Gnostic Religion. The Message of the Alien God and the Beginnings of Christianity*, Boston ²1963, London 1992

Kelly, J. N. D., *Early Christian Creeds*, London ³1972
King, K. L. (ed.), *Images of the Feminine in Gnosticism*, Philadelphia 1988
Koester, H., *Ancient Christian Gospels. Their History and Development*, London and Philadelphia 1990

Lies, L., *Origenes' 'Peri Archon'. Eine undogmatische Dogmatik*, Darmstadt 1992
Lilla, S. R. C., *Clement of Alexandria. A Study in Christian Platonism and Gnosticism*, Oxford 1971
Löhr, W. A., *Basilides und seine Schule. Eine Studie zur Theologie- und Kirchengeschichte des zweiten Jahrhunderts*, Tübingen 1996
Logan, A. H. B., review of C. Markschies, *Valentinus Gnosticus?*, *Journal of Theological Studies* 45, 1, 1994, 310–13
—, *Gnostic Truth and Christian Heresy*, Edinburgh 1996
Lüdemann, G., *Untersuchungen zur simonianischen Gnosis*, Göttingen 1975
Luttikhuizen, G. P., 'The Jewish Factor in the Development of the Gnostic Myth of Origins: Some Observations', in T. Baarda et al. (ed.), *Text and Testimony. Essays in Honour of A. F. J. Klijn*, Kampen 1988, 152–61

MacRae, C. W., *Studies in the New Testament and Gnosticism*, Wilmington, DE 1987
Marcovich, M., *Hippolytus. Refutatio omnium haeresium*, Berlin and New York 1986
Markschies, C., 'Die Krise einer philosophischen Theologie', in R. Berlinger and W. Schader (eds), *Gnosis und Philosophie: Miscellanea*, Amsterdam 1994, 227–269
—, *Valentinus Gnosticus? Untersuchungen zur valentinianischen Gnosis mit einem Kommentar zu den Fragmenten Valentins*, Tübingen 1992
Méhat, A., '"Vraie" et "fausse" gnose d'après Clément

d'Alexandrie', in B. Layton (ed.), *The Rediscovery of Gnosticism I. The School of Valentinus*, Leiden 1980, 426–33

Meijering, E. P., *Die Hellenisierung des Christentums im Urteil Adolf von Harnacks*, Amsterdam, Oxford and New York 1985

Ménard, J., *La gnose de Philon d'Alexandrie*, Paris 1987

—, *Le traité sur la résurrection (NH I, 4)*, Quebec 1983

Mortley, R., '"The Name of the Father is the Son" (Gospel of Truth 38)', in R. T. Wallis and J. Bregman (eds), *Neoplatonism and Gnosticism*, New York 1992, 239–52

Pearson, B. A., *Gnosticism, Judaism, and Egyptian Christianity*, Minneapolis 1990

—, 'Philo and Gnosticism', in H. Temporini and W. Haase (eds), *Aufstieg und Niedergang der Römischen Welt* II, 21, 1, Berlin and New York 1984, 295–342

Pétrement, S., *Le Dieu séparé. Les origines du gnosticisme*, Paris 1984

Places, É. des, *Numénius. Fragments*, Paris 1973

Poirier, P. H., *L'hymne de la perle des Actes de Thomas. Introduction, texte, traduction, commentaire*, Louvain-la-Neuve 1981

Quispel, G., 'Ezekiel 1:26 in Jewish Mysticism and Gnosis', *Vigiliae Christianae* 34, 1980, 1–13

Rizzerio, L., 'Aspects de l'évolution de la notion de *nous* dans la philosophie grecque jusqu'à Clément d'Alexandrie', in A. van Tongerloo (ed.), *The Manichaean Nous*, Louvain 1995, 219–53

Robinson, J. M. (ed.), *The Nag Hammadi Library in English*, Leiden ⁴1996

Robinson, W. C, 'The Expository Treatise on the Soul', in: B. Layton (ed.), *Nag Hammadi Codex II, 2–7* II, Leiden 1989, 136–69

Roukema, R., *De uitleg van Paulus' eerste brief aan de Corinthiërs in de tweede en derde eeuw*, Kampen 1996

—, 'Die Liebe kommt nie zu Fall (I Korinther 13, 8a) als Argument des Origenes gegen einen neuen Abfall der Seelen von Gott', in W. A. Bienert and U. Kühneweg (eds), *Origeniana Septima*, Louvain 1999

—, 'Het zelfbewustzijn van een bespotte minderheid. De receptie en uitleg van I Kor. 1:26–28 in de tweede en derde eeuw', in F. de Lange (ed.), *Geloven in de minderheid?*, Kampen 1994, 37–52

—, 'La prédication du Christ crucifié (I Corinthiens 2, 2) selon

Origène', in G. Dorival and A. le Boulluec (eds), *Origeniana Sexta*, Louvain 1995, 523–9

—, 'Reïncarnatie in de oude kerk' I-II, *Gereformeerd Theologische Tijdschrift* 92, 1992, 199–218; 93, 1993, 33–56

Rousseau, A., Doutreleau, L., et al., *Irénée de Lyon. Contre les hérésies* I–V, Paris 1965–1982

Rowe, W. V., 'Adolf von Harnack and the Concept of Hellenization', in W. E. Helleman (ed.), *Hellenization Revisited. Shaping a Christian Response within the Greco-Roman World*, Lanham, MA 1994, 69–98

Rudolph, K., *Die Gnosis*, Göttingen ³1994

—, '"Gnosis" and "Gnosticism" – The Problems of their Definition and their Relation to the Writings of the New Testament', in A. H. B. Logan and A. J. M. Wedderburn (eds), *The New Testament and Gnosis. Essays in Honour of R. McL. Wilson*, Edinburgh 1983, 21–37

Runia, D. T., *Philo of Alexandria and the Timaeus of Plato*, Leiden ²1986

Schneemelcher, W., and Wilson, R. McL., *The New Testament Apocrypha, 1. Gospels*, Louisville, Ky and Cambridge 1991

Scopello, M., *L'exégèse de l'âme. Nag Hammadi Codex II, 6. Introduction, traduction et commentaire*, Leiden 1985

Segal, A. F., *Two Powers in Heaven. Early Rabbinic Reports about Christianity and Gnosticism*, Leiden 1977

Sevrin, J. M., *L'exégèse de l'âme (NH II, 6)*, Quebec 1983

Sfameni Gasparro, G., 'Il "Vangelo secondo Filippo": rassegno degli studi e proposte di interpretazione', in W. Haase and H. Temporini (eds), *Aufstieg und Niedergang der Römischen Welt* II, 25, 6, Berlin and New York 1988, 4107–166

Shellrude, G. M., 'The Apocalypse of Adam: Evidence for a Christian Gnostic Provenance', in M. Krause (ed.), *Gnosis and Gnosticism. Papers read at the Eighth International Conference on Patristic Studies*, Leiden 1981, 82–91

Simon, M., 'Éléments gnostiques chez Philon', in U. Bianchi (ed.), *Le origini dello gnosticismo*, Leiden 1967, 359–374

Smith, M., 'The History of the Term Gnostikos', in: B. Layton (ed.), *The Rediscovery of Gnosticism. Proceedings of the International Conference on Gnosticism at Yale* II, Leiden 1981, 796–807

Smith, R., 'Sex Education in Gnostic Schools', in K. L. King (ed.), *Images of the Feminine in Gnosticism*, Philadelphia 1988, 345–60

Stroumsa, G. A. G., *Another Seed: Studies in Gnostic Mythology*, Leiden 1984

Strutwolf, H., *Gnosis als System. Zur Rezeption der valentinianischen Gnosis bei Origenes*, Göttingen 1993

Tardieu, M., *Écrits Gnostiques. Codex de Berlin*, Paris 1984

Till, W. C., *Die gnostischen Schriften des koptischen Papyrus Berolinensis 8502*, Berlin ²1972

—, *Die Pistis Sophia. Die beiden Bücher des Jeû. Unbekanntes altgnostisches Werk*, Berlin ³1959, 1962

Trigg, J. W., 'Origen Man of the Church', in R. D. Daly (ed.), *Origeniana Quinta*, Louvain 1992, 51–6

Tuckett, C. M., 'The Gospel of Thomas: Evidence for Jesus?', *Nederlands Theologisch Tijdschrift* 52, 1998, 17–32

Turcan, R., *Mithras Platonicus. Recherches sur l'hellénisation philosophique de Mithra*, Leiden 1975

Unnik, W. C. van, 'Die jüdischen Komponente in der Entstehung der Gnosis', *Vigiliae Christianae* 15, 1961, 65–82

Völker, W., *Der wahre Gnostiker nach Clemens Alexandrinus*, Berlin 1952

Vogel, C. J., *Plato. De filosoof van het transcendentie*, Baarn ²1974

Waldstein, M., and Wisse, F. (eds), *The Apocryphon of John: Synopsis of Nag Hammadi Codices II, 1; III, 1; and IV, 1 with BG 8502, 2*, Leiden 1995

Welburn, A. J., 'Reconstructing the Ophite Diagram', *Novum Testamentum* 23, 1981, 261–87

Whittaker, J., and Louis, P., *Alcinoos. Enseignement des doctrines de Platon*, Paris 1990

Widengren, G., *Mani und der Manichäismus*, Stuttgart 1961

Williams, M. A., *Rethinking 'Gnosticism'. An Argument for Dismantling a Dubious Category*, Princeton 1996

Witte, B., *Das Ophitendiagramm nach Origenes' Contra Celsum VI, 22–38*, Altenberge 1993

Wolfson, H. A., *Philo* I, Cambridge, Mass. ³1962

Zandee, J., 'Het Hermetisme en het oude Egypte', in G. Quispel (ed.), *De Hermetische Gnosis in de loop der eeuwen*, Baarn 1992, 96–174

Zehnpfennig, B., *Platon zur Einführung*, Hamburg 1997

Notes

1. Introduction

1. In this book I use the term 'catholic' ('universal') to some degree anachronistically for the 'great church' of this time (so called by the philosopher Celsus in Origen, *Against Celsus* V, 59); see J. N. D. Kelly, *Early Christian Creeds* ³1972, 385. The Orthodox churches, the Roman Catholic church and the Protestant churches go back to this catholic church of the first centuries. The Protestant term for it is 'universal Christian church'.

2. Around 150 Justin Martyr indicated in his *First Apology* 26, 8 that he had written a work against all the existing heresies. However, this has been lost and is therefore not mentioned in the above summary of witnesses to gnosticism. Probably the later authors knew and used this writing.

2. Irenaeus on the origin of the heresies

1. *Against the Heresies* I, 22, 2.

2. Cf. K. Beyschlag, *Simon Magus und die simonianische Gnosis*, 1974; G. Lüdemann, *Untersuchungen zur simonianischen Gnosis*, 1975.

3. On Philip see Acts 6.5 and 21.8; in the latter text he is called the 'evangelist'.

4. Justin, *First Apology* 26, 2–3; cf. also his *Dialogue with the Jew Trypho* 120, 6.

5. *Against the Heresies* I, 23; see also Tertullian, *On the Soul* 34; Hippolytus, *Refutation* VI, 19, 1–20, 2; Origen, *Against Celsus* V, 62; Epiphanius, *Panarion* 21, 1–4.

6. Tertullian, *On the Soul* 34, 3. The Latin translation of Irenaeus, *Against the Heresies* I, 23, 2, can be interpreted in this way: *cognoscentem quae vult Pater eius* can be translated con-

cessively as 'although she knew what her Father wanted'. Then the difference between *facere* (make) and *generare* (bring forth, bear) becomes important: the Father wanted to make or create angels through his 'first thought', but she began to give birth to them from her own movement. Thus Lüdemann, *Untersuchungen* (n.2), 58–9; cf. also Beyschlag, *Simon Magus*, 142–3.

7. The text has been handed down in the Greek (*dia tēs idias epignōseōs*) by Hippolytus, *Refutation* VI, 19, 5. Lüdemann, *Untersuchungen* (n.2), 79, thinks that the meaning here is that redemption consists of *self-knowledge* in place of 'knowledge of himself'. This translation is possible but not probable: from the Greek text of Epiphanius, *Panarion* 21, 3, 3 it seems that 'Simon' was concerned with 'knowledge of me', i.e. of Simon.

8. This explanation is also given by Epiphanius, *Panarion* 21, 2, 4.

9. In the second and third centuries, many more legendary stories were going the rounds about Simon, whether or not accompanied by Helen; these can be found in the apocryphal Acts of Peter and in two writings which bear the name of Clement of Rome, the *Pseudo-Clementine Homilies* and *Recognitions*.

10. However, that a god could appear on earth in human form does not just suggest the New Testament, because this was generally believed in the Greek world of the time. One example of this can be found in the biblical book of the Acts of the Apostles, 14.11–12, where the inhabitants of Lystra think that Paul and Barnabas are the gods Zeus and Hermes, come down to earth in human form; cf. e.g. Ovid, *Metamorphoses* VIII, 626–724.

11. The terms 'docetic' and 'docetism' are derived from the Greek verb *dokein*, which means 'think', 'appear', 'seem'.

12. Gal. 4.21–5.1.

13. See Rom. 3.28; Gal. 2.16; 5.4–5; Eph. 2.8; Titus 3.4–5.

14. Thus literally in Justin, *First Apology* 64, 5; cf. Epiphanius, *Panarion* 21.3, 4; other texts in Lüdemann, *Untersuchungen*, 55–6.

15. *Phaedo* 114bc; *Cratylus* 400bc; *Republic* 613a–621d; *Timaeus* 41d–52b.

16. *Phaedrus* 243 ab; *Republic* 586c.

17. Irenaeus, *Against the Heresies* I, 23, 5; see also already Justin, *First Apology* 26, 4; also Tertullian, *On the Soul* 50, 2–5; Epiphanius, *Panarion* 22.

18. See for example John 3.15–17; 5.24; 6.40; 6.47; 10.28; 17.2–3.

19. See Rom. 6.3; Gal. 3.27.
20. *Against the Heresies* I, 24, 1; I, 29, 1; II, *praefatio* 1; III, 4, 3; III, 11, 2.

3. *A sermon from the Nag Hammadi books*

1. The text is in the Nag Hammadi Codex II, 6, 127–37. J. N. Sevrin, *L'exégèse de l'âme (NH II, 6)*, 1983, 59–60, dates this writing between 120 and 135; W. C. Robinson, 'The Expository Treatise on the Soul' (1989), dates it to 200 at the earliest. There is an English translation (by W.C.Robinson) in J. M. Robinson (ed.), *The Nag Hammadi Library in English*, ⁴1996, 192–8.
2. There are quotations from Jer. 3.1–4; Hos. 2.1–6; Ezek. 16.23–26 in the Septuagint version (the Greek translation of the Old Testament, here translated into Coptic).
3. Thus in Acts 15.20; I Cor. 6.18; quotations of ICor. 5.9–10 and Eph. 6.12 are given.
4. At this time the male and the female sexual organs were thought to be identical, except that those of the man were external and those of the woman turned inwards. When in this Exegesis the womb of the soul is turned outwards, this indicates that she was in active search of partners. See R.Smith, 'Sex Education in Gnostic Schools', 1988, 349, 354–5.
5. Gen. 2.24.
6. Cf. John 6.63.
7. Ps. 45.11–12; Gen. 12.1.
8. Psalm 103.1–5 is quoted.
9. The words 'of God' are illegible in the Coptic text, but it is clear that the damaged part must be filled in this way; other possibilities are 'of the Father' or 'of the Spirit'.
10. A free quotation of John 6.44.
11. *Odyssey* IV, 261–4 (for this Helen see 15f. above). The words of Odysseus are not a literal quotation.
12. Cf. Sevrin, *Exégèse* (n.1), 26–9; M. Scopello, *L'exégèse de l'âme*, 1985, 144.
13. Thus for example in the Secret Book of John (NHC II, 1, 21, 11), where 'robbers' denotes the angels who imprisoned Adam in an earthly body; cf. p. 44 below, but there I am discussing another version of the Secret Book (BG 8502) in which the term 'robbers' does not appear.
14. Plotinus, *Enneads* VI, 9, 9, in the translation by A. H.

Armstrong, *Plotinus* VII. *Enneads* VI, 6–9, Cambridge, Mass.
and London 1988, 337. Cf. S.Arai, 'Simonianische Gnosis und
die *Exegese über die Seele'*, 1977, 201–2.

4. Refinements of the gnostic myth

1. Irenaeus, *Against the Heresies* I, 24, 1–2; Hippolytus, *Refutation* VII, 28. Cf. also Tertullian, *On the Soul* 23, 1; Epiphanius, *Panarion* 23.
2. This is how the Greek text runs in Hippolytus, *Refutation* VII, 28, 5 ; the Latin translation of Irenaeus here wrongly says that the powers wanted to destroy their Father.
3. See Tobit 12.15; I Enoch 20.7 (according to a Greek manuscript); 81.5.
4. Epiphanius, *Panarion* 23, 1, 7 notes that Satornilus omits the word 'our' in this text; according to the Greek translation of Gen. 1.26 God says: 'let us make a/the human being after our image and after the likeness'.
5. Irenaeus, *Against the Heresies* I, 29.
6. Irenaeus has collected many variants in his first book *Against the Heresies*. I have already discussed some simple forms of the myth, namely those of the Simonians, Menander and Satornilus.
7. There is an English translation of the long recension (by F. Wisse) in J. M. Robinson (ed.), *The Nag Hammadi Library in English*, ⁴1996, 105–23. M. Tardieu, *Écrits Gnostiques. Codex de Berlin*, 1984, 83–166, offers a French translation of the three different versions printed in parallel. I go by Tardieu's division into paragraphs. An illuminating analysis of this writing is offered by M. A. Williams, *Rethinking 'Gnosticism'*, 1996, 8–13. A study of every possible variant of the myth of this Apocryphon can be found in A. H. B. Logan, *Gnostic Truth and Christian Heresy*, 1996.
8. Similarly in, e.g., Matt. 4.21; 10.2; 20.20–24.
9. The name is clearly a reference to Ahriman, the devil in the Persian religion of Zoroastrianism, which went back to Zoroaster (Zarathustra). Compare John 8.44: according to this Gospel Jesus told 'the Jews' they were descended from the devil.
10. Cf. e.g. John 8.14; 13.3; 16.5; 16.28; 20.17.
11. It is unclear what this name means. Some possibilities are summed up by Logan, *Gnostic Truth* (n.7), 98–100.
12. A similar word play also occurs in Eph. 2.7; 4.32; Philemon 11.

13. Cf. John 1.3; Matt. 28.18.

14. In his account in *Against the Heresies* I, 29, 3, Irenaeus has kept a Greek explanation of Adam's name. In Hebrew Adam means 'human being', 'humankind'. But because with a Greek ending 'Adam' becomes 'Adamas', which means 'indomitable', 'unconquerable', this meaning is attached to his name. This explicit explanation has dropped out of the Coptic texts, but they still mention an unconquerable power.

15. It appears from the fact that the 'Self-Procreated' and the 'Son' are distinguished here that they were not originally identified, as is the case in 19 and 23.

16. According to Irenaeus, *Against the Heresies* I, 29, 4, this wish of Sophia, alias Prounikos (Greek for 'lewd', 'sensuous'), was accompanied by a leap from the Father. For this see the myth of the Simonians, above 15.

17. The first explanation would be a derivation from Yao El Sabaoth; see S.Pétrement, *Le Dieu séparé. Les origines du gnosticisme*, 1984, 70. Other explanations in Logan, *Gnostic Truth* (n.7), 126–7.

18. God's throne for example in I Kings 22.19; Pss. 45.7; 47.9; Isa. 66.1; Ezek. 1.26; the pillar of cloud which by night was a pillar of fire is in Exod. 13.21–22; 14.19; 14.24; Num. 14.14.

19. E.g. in Job 10.16; Isa. 38.13; Hos. 5.14; 11.10; 13.7–8.

20. The reading 'ignorance' in Nag Hammadi Codex III, 16, 7 and Irenaeus, *Against the Heresies* I, 29, 4. Here the Berlin Codex 39, 5 reads 'folly'.

21. Yaoth suggests Yahweh; Adonaios and Adonin suggest Adonai ('Lord'), but also the Greek god Adonis (however, this name has a Semitic origin); 'Sabaoth' means 'powers', 'hosts' and in the Old Testament is often added to the name of the Lord.

22. See the previous note. 'Sabbataios' is clearly derived from 'Sabbath' and refers to one of the commandments of the Old Testament God. Moreover 'Shabbetai' is the Hebrew name for the God Cronus/Kronos or Saturn, whose day Saturday or the sabbath is.

23. Derived from the Hebrew *sakhal* or the Aramaic *sakhla*, 'foolish'.

24. These words are taken from Exod. 20.5; Deut. 5.9 and Isa. 45.5–6; 46.9, where they are applied to the God of the Old Testament.

25. According to Irenaeus, *Against the Heresies* I, 29, 4, however,

she fled to the eighth sphere which was thus one level above the creation of Yaldabaoth, and still lay outside the fullness (the *pleroma*) of the aeons. This idea of things is probably older.

26. For this interpretation see Irenaeus, *Against the Heresies* I, 30, 6 and *The Origin of the World* (NHC II, 5) 103. For the creation of Adam's body see also R. van den Broek, *Studies in Gnosticism and Alexandrian Christianity*, 1996, 67–85.

27. See e.g. Plato, *Cratylus* 400c; *Phaedo* 114bc.

28. The plural 'them' (Berlin Codex 57, 20–58, 1) anticipates the creation of the woman, Eve, which has not yet been narrated; this passage is therefore a later addition. 'Him', Adam, stands in the longer version (Nag Hammadi Codex III, 28, 16).

29. According to the Berlin Codex 58, 4–5 the serpent taught these things to her, i.e. to the woman, although her creation has still to take place. By contrast Nag Hammadi Codex II, 22, 11 and III, 28, 19 speak of 'Adam' or 'him'.

30. That Yaldabaoth still got a portion of the power is mentioned only in the longer version, Nag Hammadi Codex II, 22, 33ff.

31. 'Yaue' and 'Eloim' are the usual names for God in the Old Testament, usually translated as 'Lord' and 'God'.

32. Cf. Matt. 12.31–32.

33. See e.g. Cicero, *Republic* VI, 16–17 (Scipio's dream; also Chapter 7, 89 and 91).

34. Bruce Codex 52.

35. For this 'docetism' see p. 20 and 179 n. 11 above.

36. First Revelation of James (Nag Hammadi Codex V, 3) 33, 34 (Coptic), English translation by W. R. Schoedel in J. M. Robinson (ed.), *The Nag Hammadi Library in English*, ⁴1996, 265–6; Irenaeus, *Against the Heresies* I, 21, 5 (Latin); Epiphanius, *Panarion* 36, 3, 2 (Greek).

37. Irenaeus, *Against the Heresies* I, 21, 5.

38. Irenaeus, *Against the Heresies* I, 30.

39. Irenaeus, *Against the Heresies* I, 30, 5; cf. 2.2.9 on pp. 41f.

40. Cf. p. 9. Origen writes about the Ophites in *Against Celsus* VI, 22–32.

41. The name Adonaios does not appear in *Against Celsus* VI, 31, but it does in VI, 32.

42. *Against Celsus* VI, 31. It is strange that Origen gives the passwords in the reverse order: he begins with the last password to the 'solitary king' and only at the end gives the password that the soul must use first. From this it has been concluded that

these passwords are not meant for the ascent of the soul after earthly life but for her descent from highest heaven to the earth (thus e.g. in B. Witte, *Das Ophitendiagramm nach Origenes' Contra Celsum VI, 22–38,* 1993, 112–22). But this interpretation, too, causes problems. The content of some passwords clearly points to a rediscovered freedom which cannot apply to a descent to the earth, but can to an ascent on high. The authors who think that the passwords are meant for a descent do not give a satisfactory interpretation of a rediscovered freedom. I therefore assume that the order in Origen's copy of the Ophite ritual has been distorted. See also A. J. Welburn, 'Reconstructing the Ophite Diagram', 1981, esp. 264.

43. The Leviathan is called a serpent in Isa. 27.1; cf. also e.g. Job 3.8; Ps. 104.25. That the Ophites perhaps put this Leviathan in the eighth sphere can be inferred from *Against Celsus* VI 25; there he is called 'soul of the universe'. For this presupposition see Witte, *Ophitendiagramm* (n.42), 115–16.

44. Origen, *Against Celsus* VI, 31. This and the previous quotations are from H. Chadwick, *Origen: Contra Celsum,* Cambridge 1965, 347.

45. Revelation of Paul (Nag Hammadi Codex V, 2) 20–23.

5. The origin and purpose of life

1. Seneca lived from about 4 BC to AD 65. He wrote the *Letters to Lucilius* in 63–64.

2. Seneca, *Letters to Lucilius* 65, 19–20. The quotations in this section are in the translation by R. M. Gummere, *Seneca ad Lucilium, Epistulae Morales* I, Loeb Classical Library, Cambridge, Mass. and London 1917, 455, 457; II, 243, 245.

3. Seneca, *Letters to Lucilius* 82, 5–6. Cf. Seneca, *Naturales quaestiones* III, *praefatio* 10–18.

4. I Clement 38.3. Translation by K. Lake, *The Apostolic Fathers* I, Loeb Classical Library, Cambridge, Mass. and London 1912, 75

5. I Clement 38.4.

6. I Clement 40.1; cf. Paul, I Corinthians 2.10 and I Peter 1.12.

7. The Mishnah is a collection of sixty-three writings about the Jewish tradition. This collection was made in Galilee around 200 by Rabbi Judah.

8. Pirke Aboth 3.1, as translated by R. Travers Herford, *The Ethics of the Talmud: Sayings of the Fathers,* New York 1962, 63.

9. Aboth de rabbi Nathan 19; Derek Eretz Zuta 3.9; Derek Eretz Rabbah 3.1 (here the text stands in the name of Simeon ben Azzai of Tiberias, from the second century); Jerusalem Talmud, Sotah 2.2.

10. Philo, *On the Cherubim* 109; 113.

11. In his edition Cohn has added *mou* (translated as 'I am') to *metastantos*; others have followed him.

12. The term for 'rebirth' (*paliggenesia*) is of Stoic origin and often refers to the rebirth of the whole world after the conflagration; it also occurs in Matt. 19.28. However, here Philo is referring only to individual life after death.

13. Philo, *On the Cherubim* 115, as translated by F. H. Colson and G. J. Whittaker, *Philo in Ten Volumes (and Two Supplementary Volumes)*, Loeb Classical Library, Cambridge, Mass. and London 1927–1953, 75–7. The last words have probably been handed down wrongly in the Greek manuscripts, namely 'with composition and quality'. Colson has corrected this to 'without composition and without quality' (*asugkritoi apoioi*); this reading has been followed by others.

14. Philo, *On the Cherubim* 115; for 'know' he uses *gnorizein* three times and *eidenai* (*oide*) once.

15. See 33, 41, 50–3. The myth of the school of Valentinus diverges in a variety of points from the myths of Satornilus and the Secret Book of John (see chapter 4). But the Valentinian myth also taught that the material world was governed by a Creator and seven angelic powers in the seven spheres of heaven; see Irenaeus, *Against the Heresies* I, 5, 2.

16. Clement of Alexandria, *Excerpts from Theodotus* 69, 1–78, 1.

17. Clement of Alexandria, *Excerpts from Theodotus* 78, 2. The term for 'rebirth' (cf. Philo, 4) here is *anagennesis*, and denotes the new life that begins with baptism. See John 3.3.

18. Tertullian, *Prescription of Heretics* 7, 1–4; 7, 6, translation by P. Holmes in A. Cleveland Coxe (ed.), *Tertullian*, The Ante-Nicene Fathers III, reissued Grand Rapids 1980, 246.

19. Tertullian, *Prescription of Heretics* 7, 5.

6. *The Jewish religion*

1. The word occurs in the Septuagint for the first time in Gen. 2.4: 'This is the book of the genesis of heaven and earth', and after that again in Gen. 5.1.

2. But some prophets do refer to the garden of Eden: Isa. 51.3; Ezek. 28.13; 31.9; 31.16–18; Joel 2.3.

3. E.g. Isa. 24.1–6; Jer. 4.23–28.

4. The Septuagint translation is 'You have made him a little lower than the angels.' This psalm displays an affinity with Gen. 1.

5. Sirach 7.15; cf. 33.10–12; 40.1. This work comes from 190–170 BCE.

6. Wisdom of Solomon 1.13–14. Cf. also 2.23–24, quoted on p. 70. The work was written in Greek and probably comes from the first century BCE.

7. Eccles.3.20; cf. Gen. 2.7; 3.19; Pss. 90.3; 104.29; 146.4.

8. See Eccles. 3.21: 'who knows whether the breath (or spirit [*ruach*]) of the children of men rises upwards and the breath of animals descends, below in the earth'; Eccles 9.10: 'in the realm of the dead there is no work, plan, knowledge or wisdom'. Cf. Ps. 6.6; 30.10; 115.17.

9. Eccles.12.7. The word 'spirit' (*ruach*) can also be translated 'breath'; cf. the previous note.

10. For exceptions like Enoch and Elijah see Gen. 5.24; II Kings 2.1–11; more generally Ps. 49.16; 73.24. See also Wisdom 2.23, quoted on p. 70.

11. Job 42.17a, clearly with reference to Job 19.26. Cf. Ps. 1.5–6; Isa. 26.19; Ezek. 37.1–14; from the second century BCE, Dan. 12.2; II Macc.7; Testament of Judah 25; Testament of Benjamin 10.6–11; Ethiopian Enoch 51; from the first century BCE, Psalms of Solomon 2.31; 3.12.

12. Testament of Job 4.9–10; 39.8–40.3; 52.1–12 (from the beginning of our era).

13. Deut. 6.4; cf. 4.34–35. In Job 16.20–21 Job makes a distinction between the God on whom he calls and the God who torments him, but without assailing the unity of God.

14. Isa. 45.5; cf. Isa. 43.10–12; 44.6–8; 44.24; 46.9.

15. Cf. I Sam. 5.1–4; Isa. 44.6–20; Ps. 115.4–7. That over the centuries Israel was not as monotheistic as has often been assumed is argued by M. Barker, *The Great Angel. A Study of Israel's Second God*, 1992.

16. Gen. 6.2; Job 1.6; 2.1; 38.7.

17. E.g. I Sam. 16.14–16; 18.10; I Kings 22.19–23.

18. Job 1.6–12; 2.1–8; I Chron. 21.1 (cf. II Sam. 24.1); Zech. 3.1–2.

19. See e.g. Deut. 32.8 in the Septuagint (the Most High 'set the bounds of the nations according to the number of the angels of

God'); Dan. 10.13; 10.20–21 (from the second century BCE); Tobit 3.8; 5.4; 6.8; 8.3; 12.15.

20. Gen. 6.1–4; Ethiopian Enoch 6–9 (from the second or first century BCE). Cf. in the New Testament II Peter 2.4; Jude 6.

21. Life of Adam and Eve 12–16 (from the first century CE). Cf. in the New Testament Luke 10.18; Rev.12.7–12.

22. Barker, *The Great Angel* (n.15), 48–69, thinks that this wisdom is a manifestation of the earlier mother goddess who was worshipped in Israel.

23. Proverbs 8.22–31. Since in Proverbs 1.5; 4.5–7; 16.16; 17.16 *qānāh* occurs in connection with wisdom and insight in the sense of 'acquire', there is reason also to translate it this way in 8.22. Thus in the translations of Aquila, Symmachus, Theodotion and in Philo, *On Drunkenness* 31 (cf. p. 86). But *qānāh* can also mean 'create' and is thus translated in the (influential) Septuagint.

24. For example Sirach 1.1–10; 4.11–19; 24.1–22; Baruch 3.9–38 (wisdom 'appeared on earth and lived among men'); also in the Hebrew book Job 28.12–28.

25. Wisdom 7.25–26.

26. Wisdom 1.4–7; 9.17.

27. Wisdom 10.1–2. The term for 'transgression' (*paraptōma*) can also be translated 'fall'.

28. Wisdom 9.4.

29. Wisdom 18.14–15. According to 7.23 Wisdom is also 'all-powerful' (*pantodynamos*). For this 'Word' of God see in the Hebrew Bible: Ps. 33.6; 147.15–18; Isa. 55.11; Jer. 23.29.

30. Ezek. 1.26. Cf. G. Quispel, 'Ezekiel 1, 26 in Jewish Mysticism and Gnosis', 1980.

31. This text can be found in Eusebius, *Preparation for the Gospel* IX, 29.

32. Dan. 7.9; 7.13–14.

33. Ethiopian Enoch 46.1–5; 48.2; 62.5–14.

34. Babylonian Talmud Hagigah 14bc; 15a.

35. For this see A. F. Segal, *Two Powers in Heaven. Early Rabbinic Reports about Christianity and Gnosticism*, 1977.

36. E.g. Ps. 94.10 (Ps. 93 in the LXX); 119.66 (Ps. 118 in the LXX); Prov. 8.9–12; 21.11; Eccles 1.16–18; 2.26; Hos. 4.6; 10.12 (in the LXX).

37. Cf. R. Bultmann, in *TDNT* I, 700–1.

38. Dan. 12.4; *gnosis* in the Greek translation by Theodotion. For

the relationship between apocalyptic and gnosticism see I. Gruenwald, *From Apocalypticism to Gnosticism*, 1988.

39. Community Rule (1QS) 4.4; 4.6 (from the second century BCE).

7. Plato, Philo and Platonic philosophy

1. For 'knowledge' Plato usually uses the term *epistēmē*, but also *gnosis*; cf. for example *Republic* 476c–478c; 484c; 508e; 527b. Plato uses the term 'gnostic' to differentiate between theoretical ('gnostic') and practical knowledge; thus in *Statesman* 258e–261b.

2. *Theaetetus* 155d.

3. For this see his *Letter* VII, 341b–344d.

4. See *Euthyphro* 2a–3b; *Apology* 23cd; 24bc.

5. *Phaedo* 64c–69c; 80a; initially the term for 'forms' does not occur here in its specific meaning of 'ideas' (but cf. 79ab); however, it does appear later in 102a, 103e. See also *Cratylus* 439c–440b; *Parmenides* 128e–135c; *Symposium* 211a–212b; *Phaedrus* 246a–247e; *Meno* 73e–76e; *Republic* 517b–520c; 596b–597e; *Timaeus* 51b–e.

6. *Theaetetus* 176b; cf. *Republic* 613a.

7. For this see already pp. 20f.

8. *Phaedo* 72e–77a; *Phaedrus* 249c–250c; *Meno* 81c–85d; *Republic* 619e–621d; cf. also Socrates' role as 'midwife' according to *Theaetetus* 149a–151b.

9. *Philebus* 28c–31a; cf. *Phaedo* 97c–98b; *Phaedrus* 247cd; *Republic* 596cd.

10. *Timaeus* 30ab; 39e; 46b–47b.

11. *Republic* 502d–509c; 517b–521b.

12. *Symposium* 210e–212b; *Parmenides* 137c–166c.

13. See pp. 91f.

14. For this see also *Republic* 379a–380c.

15. On this see D. T. Runia, *Philo of Alexandria and the Timaeus of Plato*, ²1986.

16. See *On Noah's Work as a Planter* 18–20.

17. *On the Confusion of Tongues* 168–182; *On Flight and Finding* 68–72; *On the Change of Names*, 30–32; *On the Special Laws* I, 45–49; cf. *On the Eternity of the World* 13.

18. *On the Special Laws* I, 327–329; *On the Confusion of Tongues* 172; *Questions on Exodus* I, 23.

19. Cf. p. 68.

20. *On the Creation*, 171; cf. Deut. 6.4.

21. *On the Creation*, 21. Cf. for the 'the true Good' 1.4 (p. 80).

22. *On the Cherubim* 27–28; cf. *On the Sacrifices of Abel and Cain* 59.

23. In Exod. 3.14 the name of God (translated from the Hebrew) is: 'I am who I am' or 'I shall be who I shall be'. In the Greek of the Septuagint these words are translated 'I am the Existent'.

24. *Who is the Heir* 166; *Allegorical Interpretation* I, 96; III, 73; *Noah's Work as a Planter* 86; *Flight and Finding* 94–98; *Change of Names* 11–14, 28–29; *On Abraham* 121–124; *On Moses* I, 75–76; II, 99–100; *Questions on Exodus* II, 68.

25. *Allegorical Interpretation* III, 207: Deut. 6.13 is quoted; cf. *On Dreams* I, 227–230; *Questions on Genesis* II, 62.

26. *On Drunkenness* 30–31; *On Flight and Finding* 109. For Prov. 8.22 cf. 187 n. 23. Also *Cherubim* 49–50; *The Worse attacks the Better* 54, 115–116.

27. *On the Giants* 12–15; *Noah's Work as a Planter* 14; *Confusion of Tongues* 77–8; *Who is the Heir* 239–40, 282–3.

28. *On Dreams* I, 138–139; cf. *Noah's Work as a Planter* 14; *Posterity of Cain* 124.

29. *On Rewards and Punishments* 9; *On Moses* I, 21; *Change of Names* 100–101; *On Dreams* II, 294.

30. *Who is the Heir* 308–309.

31. *On the Unchangeableness of God* 143; cf. *Allegorical Interpretation* III, 126; *Flight and Finding* 82; *On Abraham* 268; *On the Virtues* 178–179.

32. See e.g. the Handbook (*Didaskalikos*) of the teaching of Plato 1–3; I am using the edition with a French translation by J. Whittaker and P. Louis 1990. The references in the main text are to the chapters of this Handbook.

33. I am following the edition and numbering of É. des Places 1973. This is more selective in its collection of fragments than the previous edition by E. A. Leemans (1937). See also M. Baltes, 'Numenios von Apamea und der platonische Timaios', 1975.

34. Fr. 43; 52. In fr.52 (taken from Calcidius, *Commentary on the Timaeus* 295–299), Numenius refers to Plato, *Laws* 896e and 897d, which speaks of a good and a bad soul of the world. Numenius interprets the bad world soul as matter.

35. Fr. 35, where Numenius offers a very free exposition of Plato, *Republic* 616c. For this interpretation see A. J. Festugière, *Proclus. Commentaire sur la République* III, 1970, 72–4 (Proclus, *Commentary on Plato's Republic* XVI, 128–32).

36. Fr. 33. R. Turcan, *Mithras Platonicus. Recherches sur l'hellénisation philosophique de Mithra*, 1975, 49, thinks that fr. 12 is also about reincarnation.

8. The mystery religions and early Christianity

1. For the text see Plutarch, *Moralia*, translated by F. C. Babbitt *et al.*, Loeb Classical Library, Vol.5, Cambridge, Mass. and London 1936.

2. Plutarch, *Isis and Osiris* 12–18 (*Moralia* 355d–358b). In passing, Plutarch mentions the tradition that afterwards Typho procreated 'Jerusalem and Jew' (31/363d).

3. *Isis and Osiris* 53–58 (*Moralia* 372e–375a).

4. *Isis and Osiris* 78 (*Moralia* 382e–383a).

5. *Isis and Osiris* 1–2 (*Moralia* 351c–352a). Plutarch connects *isis* with *eidenai*, 'know', and analyses *iseion* into *eisomenos*, 'he who shall know', and *to on*, 'the being'. However, Plutarch also offers other explanations of the name Isis; cf. 60 (*Moralia* 375cd).

6. *Isis and Osiris* 1; cf. 11; 35 (*Moralia* 351c, 355b, 364e).

7. A book by Lucian of Samosata from the second century about the adventures of this Lucius is also known. However, worship of Isis does not occur in it.

8. Apuleius, *Metamorphoses* (The Golden Ass), III, 24–25.

9. The translation is that of J. A. Hanson, Apuleius, *Metamorphoses* II, Loeb Classical Library, Cambridge, Mass. and London 1989, 305.

10. *Metamorphoses* I, 8–20; II, 5; III, 15–18; VI, 1–5; VIII, 24–30; IX, 8–10; IX, 14–16; X, 33.

11. There is a survey of the very different views of Jesus in C. J. den Heyer, *Jesus Matters*, London 1997.

12. Matt. 1.1–25; 3.17; 5.44–45; 6.25–34; 11.25–27; Luke 1.26–38; 2.6–7; John 3.16–18.

13. Matt. 4.23–9.35; 11.16–24; 22.37–40; Luke 3.23; 4.18–19.

14. Luke 11.52.

15. Matt. 10.1–4; 26.47–27.50.

16. Matt. 16.21; 17.22–23; 20.17–19; 26.2; 28.1–20; Luke 24; John 20–21.

17. Matt. 20.28; 26.28; John 1.29; I Cor. 15.3; II Cor. 5.17–21; Heb. 9.24–28; I John 1.7–2.2; 4.10.

18. Luke 24.31; 24.36–43; John 20.19–29; I Cor. 15.5–8.

19. Especially in the Gospels of Matthew and John and in the Letter

to the Hebrews; cf. also Luke 24.27; Acts 2.25–36; I Cor. 15.3–4; Gal. 3.13.

20. Matt. 9.6; 16.16; 26.63–64; John 1.41; 1.51.
21. Rom. 10.9; I Cor. 12.3; Phil. 2.11.
22. John 1.1–4; 1.14–18; cf. I John 4.3; II John 7; Ignatius, Ephesians superscription; 7.2; Trallians 9.
23. John 3.13; 3.31–34; 6.38; 20.17; Acts 1.9–11; Phil. 2.5–11.
24. Matt. 24.30; 26.64; John 5.25–29; I Cor. 15.20–28; Phil. 3.20–21.
25. II Cor. 5.1–10; Phil. 1.23; II Tim. 4.18; Rev.5.11; 7.4–17; cf. John 14.1–3.
26. Matt. 26.64; John 20.22; Acts 2–3; 8–9.
27. Acts 6.6–15; 8.4–11.26; 15.1–5; 21.17–26.
28. Rom. 3.21–30; 5.1–11; 6.1–4; 10.4–13. Cf. John 10.16; Eph. 2.11–22.
29. Cf. Acts 15.1–29; I Cor. 7.18–19; Gal. 6.12–13; Col. 2.16–23.
30. This is evident, for example, from Gal. 5.2–4; I Tim. 1.7; Titus 3.9; Ignatius, Magn.8.1; 9.1; 10.3; in these texts Christians who held more to Judaism are challenged.
31. Heb. 8.13; Barnabas 14.1–6; 15.5–16.2.
32. Rom. 11.33; 15.14; I Cor. 1.5; 8.7–11; 12.8; 13.2; 13.8; 14.6; II Cor. 2.14; 4.6; 8.7; 10.5; 11.6; Phil. 3.8.
33. I Cor. 8.1.
34. Eph. 3.19; II Peter 1.5–6; 3.18; Didache 9.3; 10.2; 11.2; I Clem.1.2; 36.2; 40.1; 41.4; 48.5; Ignatius, Eph. 17.2; Barnabas 1.5; 2.3, etc.
35. John 14.5–7; cf. 6.69; 8.28; 8.32; 10.38; 14.20; 17.25–26.
36. John 17.3; 20.31.

9. A form of Hellenized Christianity

1. Cf. G. W. MacRae, *Studies in the New Testament and Gnosticism*, 1987, 184–202, and the critical review by G. P. Luttikhuizen, 'The Jewish Factor in the Development of the Gnostic Myth of Origins: Some Observations', 1988.
2. That Yaldabaoth is a Hebrew divine name holds only if the explanation 'Lord God of the powers' (or something similar, see p. 41) is correct.
3. The term Lawgiver (*nomothetēs*) for God does not occur in the Septuagint but in Philo, *Sacrifices of Abel and Cain* 131; *Flight and Finding* 66, 99; *Moses* II, 48; and once in the New Testament, in James 4.12.

4. That the gnostics took their view of reincarnation from Plato is also stated by the Neoplatonic philosopher Plotinus, *Enneads* II, 9, 6.

5. This is not true of all 'gnostic' texts; see the discussion of the Gospel of Truth and the Treatise on the Resurrection in Chapter 11, 3 and 4.

6. A number of Old Testament psalms are also quoted and explained in a gnostic way in the *Pistis Sophia*.

7. See also the discussion of Ptolemaeus' Letter to Flora in Chapter 10. 4.

8. See G. W. Macrae, *Studies in the New Testament and Gnosticism*, 1987, 256; he refers to the Gospel of Philip (NHC II, 3) 53–54; 66 and to The Thunder: Perfect Mind (NHC VI, 2) 14 and 19 as texts in which good and bad are radically relativized. However, the question is whether these texts can be interpreted as a licence for loose living.

9. See for example Irenaeus, *Against the Heresies* I, 6, 3; 13, 3–7; 23, 4; 25, 3–5; II, 32, 1–2; Clement, *Stromateis*, III, 40; Epiphanius, *Panarion* 26, 3, 3; 26, 4–5; 26, 9, 6–9; 26, 17, 4; Plotinus, *Enneads* II, 9, 15–17; cf. A. le Boulluec, *La notion d'hérésie dans la littérature grecque IIe –IIIe siècles* I, 1985, 114–35.

10. See M. A. Williams, *Rethinking 'Gnosticism'. An Argument for Dismantling a Dubious Category*, 1996, 96–162; P. Brown, *The Body and Society. Men, Women and Sexual Renunciation in Early Christianity*, 1989.

11. See Justin, *First Apology* 26, 7; 27, 5; *Second Apology* 12, 1–2; Athenagoras, *Supplication* 3; Minucius Felix, *Octavius* 9; Tertullian, *Apologeticum* 7–8.

12. For example Hos. 5.14; 11.10; 13.7–8 (cf. p. 41).

13. Exod. 20.5; 34.14; Deut. 4.24; 5.9; 6.15 (cf. p. 42). The Hebrew word *qanna*, 'envious', 'jealous', is translated in the Septuagint as *zelotes*, which means 'zealous'. But the Septuagint term (which is often used by gnostics) can also be translated as 'jealous', see A. Le Boulluec and P. Sandevoir, *La Bible d'Alexandrie 2, L'Exode*, 1989, 206.

14. Isa. 45.5–6; 46.9 (cf. p. 42).

15. For this 'heretical' view (or misunderstanding, from the catholic perspective) of the Old Testament see the reactions of some church fathers: Clement of Alexandria, *Tutor* I, 68, 2–3; *Selections from the Prophets* 26, 1; Origen, *On the Principles* II,

5, 1–3; IV, 2, 1; *Homilies on Exodus* 8.5; *Commentary on Matthew* XVII, 19. Augustine, too, initially had a great deal of difficulty with the Old Testament, as emerges from his *Confessions* V, 14, 24.

16. The church fathers and the philosopher Plotinus also point to the philosophical background of gnosticism; see for example Irenaeus, *Against the Heresies* II, 14, 1–6; Tertullian, *Prescription of Heretics* 7, 2–11; Hippolytus, *Refutation* V, 2; VI, 3; VI, 21–29; VII, 14–20; Plotinus, *Enneads* II, 9, 6; 9, 17.

17. Cf. e.g. the Apocalypse of Adam (NHC V, 5). But Christian elements can also be recognized here; cf. G. M. Shellrude, 'The Apocalypse of Adam: Evidence for a Christian Gnostic Provenance?', 1981, and G. A. G. Stroumsa, *Another Seed: Studies in Gnostic Mythology*, 1984, 81–113.

18. Cf. G. P. Luttikhuizen, 'The Jewish Factor' (n.1), but he thinks that the myth cannot have arisen in a Jewish milieu; he attributes the use of facts from the Old Testament to Christians.

19. Cf. Irenaeus, *Against the Heresies* I, praefatio 1.

20. This can be inferred from, e.g. Irenaeus, *Against the Heresies* III, 16, 1; Tertullian, *Against the Valentinians* 1, 4.

21. Origen, *Against Celsus* III, 12. Translation by Henry Chadwick, *Origen: Contra Celsum*, Cambridge 1965, 135–6.

22. I would recall (cf. p. 82 above) that Philo's Middle Platonism does not derive only from Plato but also underwent the influence of Aristotle and the Stoics.

23. Thus in Corpus Hermeticum I (this first chapter is also called Poimandres).

24. Cf. J. Zandee, 'Het Hermetisme en het oude Egypte', 1992; C. H. Dodd, *The Bible and the Greeks*, ³1964, 99–248; B. A. Pearson, *Gnosticism, Judaism, and Egyptian Christianity*, 1990, 136–47.

25. For this see the discussion of Clement of Alexandria and Origen in Chapter 12.

26. See U. Bianchi (ed.), *Le origini dello gnosticismo*, 1967, xx-xxxii.

27. See M.Smith, 'The History of the Term Gnostikos' (1981).

28. Ibid., 801–6.

29. See Chapter 12, 1.

30. William, *Rethinking 'Gnosticism'* (n.10), 51–3; see n.27 for Smith's article.

31. Thus H. Jonas, *The Gnostic Religion*, ²1963.

32. Cf. K. Rudolph, '"Gnosis" and "Gnosticism" – The Problems of their Definition and their Relation to the Writings of the New Testament', 1983.

33. In Williams' proposal to speak of 'biblical demiurgical traditions' there is inevitably also a lack of clarity about the demarcation. 'Biblical demiurgical traditions' do not explicitly occur in the 'Exegesis on the Soul', but they are probably implicit. What does this mean for the classification of this writing, which does seem to be akin to other 'biblical demiurgical traditions'?

34. Thus J. Ménard, *La gnose de Philon d'Alexandrie*, 1987.

35. A. von Harnack. *Lehrbuch der Dogmengeschichte* I, ⁵1931, 250. E. P. Meijering, *Die Hellenisierung des Christentums im Urteil Adolf von Harnacks*, 1985, gives a good account of this topic and of the changes that Harnack made after the appearance of the first edition (of 1885) (for Gnosticism see 22–3, 54–6, 80–5, 106–8).

36. See W. V. Rowe, 'Adolf von Harnack and the Concept of Hellenization', 1994.

10. Some gnostic and related teachers

1. Irenaeus, *Against the Heresies* I, 26, 1; III, 11, 1.

2. Hippolytus, *Refutation* VII, 33; X, 21.

3. Irenaeus, *Against the Heresies* III, 3, 4; Eusebius, *Church History* IV, 14, 6.

4. Irenaeus, *Against the Heresies* III, 11, 1; cf. John 1.1–5.

5. The testimonies about Basilides and the fragments of his work have been collected with a commentary by W. A. Löhr, *Basilides und seine Schule*, 1996.

6. Clement, *Stromateis* II, 10; 27, 2; 36, 1; IV, 81–83; 86, 1; 153, 4; 165, 3; V, 3, 2; 74, 3; VII, 106, 4; *Excerpts from Theodotus*, 28; Hippolytus, *Refutation* VII, 20, 1.

7. Clement, *Stromateis* III, 1–3.

8. For Hippolytus see *Refutation* VII, 20–27; X, 14; Löhr, *Basilides* (n.5), 284–323.

9. Irenaeus, *Against the Heresies* I, 24, 3–7; cf. Löhr, *Basilides* (n.5), 256–73.

10. See Löhr, *Basilides* (n.5), 331–2.

11. See Irenaeus, *Against the Heresies* I, 11, 1; III, 4, 3; Clement, *Stromateis* VII, 106, 3–4; Tertullian, *Against the Valentinians* 4, 1; Epiphanius, *Panarion* 31, 2, 1–3; 7, 1–2; Eusebius, *Church*

History IV, 11, 1.

12. C. Markschies, *Valentinus Gnosticus?*, 1992; all the fragments of Valentinus are collected and discussed in this book. There is also a brief survey in C. Markschies, 'Die Krise einer philosophischen Theologie', 1994.

13. Clement, *Stromateis* II, 36, 2–4; see Markschies, *Valentinus* (n.12), 11–53.

14. Clement, *Stromateis* III, 59, 3; see Markschies, *Valentinus* (n.12), 83–117.

15. Irenaeus, *Against the Heresies* I, 11, 1; also in Epiphanius, *Panarion* 31, 32.

16. Tertullian, *Against the Valentinians* 4, 1; 4, 3 ('for they have deviated from the founder'; 'so Valentinus is no longer anywhere, yet they are Valentinians, and indeed through Valentinus'); see Markschies, *Valentinus* (n.12), 302–3, 392–402.

17. Thus A. H. B. Logan in his review of Markschies' book, 1994; G. Quispel, 'Valentinus and the Gnostikoi', 1996.

18. Clement, *Stromateis* II, 10, 2.

19. Ireaneus, *Against the Heresies* I, praefatio 2; cf. Tertullian, *Against the Valentinians* 4, 2.

20. Hippolytus, *Refutation* VI 35, 5–6. According to Hippolytus, this Italian tendency thought that Jesus first had a 'psychic' body ('a soul body'), which means that it initially lacked the Spirit, and that the Spirit, or the Logos of Sophia, had descended on it at his baptism.

21. Irenaeus, *Against the Heresies* I, 1–9.

22. Epiphanius, *Panarion* 33, 3–8.

23. Clement, *Stromateis* IV, 71, 1; Hippolytus, *Refutation* VI, 35, 5–6; there is a survey of Heracleon's work and views in C. P. Bammel, *Tradition and Exegesis in Early Christian Writers*, 1995, IV.

24. Origen, *Commentary on John* II, 73–75, 100–104.

25. Hippolytus, *Refutation* VI, 35, 5–6; cf. n.20.

26. Clement, *Extracts from Theodotus*, 58–60; cf. 1, 1; 35, 1–2.

27. Ibid., 61–62.

28. Hippolytus, *Refutation* V, 23–27.

29. See respectively K.Rudolph, *Die Gnosis* ³1994, 159; M. A. Williams, *Rethinking 'Gnosticism'*, 1996, 18.

30. See R. van den Broek, *Studies in Gnosticism and Alexandrian Christianity*, 1996, 131–41.

31. Hippolytus, *Refutation* V, 27, 5.
32. See Justin, *First Apology* 26, 2–5; Irenaeus, *Against the Heresies* II, 31, 1; III, 4, 3; IV, 6, 4; Tertullian, *Prescription of Heretics* 30, 1–3; Clement, *Stromateis* VII, 106, 4–107, 1; Epiphanius, *Panarion* 42, 1, 3–4. The sources on Marcion have been collected by A. von Harnack, *Marcion*, 1924, 3*–30*.
33. Irenaeus, *Against the Heresies* III, 3, 4; Eusebius, *Church History* IV, 14, 7.
34. Irenaeus, *Against the Heresies* I, 27, 1; IV, 33, 2; Epiphanius, *Panarion* 41, 1, 1–9; 42, 1, 4; Harnack, *Marcion*, 23–24; 25*–26*.
35. Tertullian, *Against Marcion*, I, 11, 9; II, 5, 1; II, 9, 1; V, 6, 11.
36. See B. Aland, 'Marcion. Versuch einer neuen Interpretation', 1973, 434.
37. Tertulian, *Against Marcion* III, 8, 2–7.
38. Origen, *Homilies on Exodus* 6, 9; also Harnack, *Marcion* (n.32), 132–3, 288*.
39. Irenaeus, *Against the Heresies* I, 27, 3.
40. Tertullian, *Against Marcion* I, 19, 4.
41. The remains of Marcion's texts have been collected in Harnack, *Marcion* (n.32), 40*–313*.
42. Ibid., 148–9; 277*–288*.
43. See John 14.16; 14.26; 15.26; 16.7.
44. These sources have been handed down in a great many languages such as Coptic, Syriac, Arabic, Persian, Greek and Latin. For this survey of Mani's life and teaching I have made use of G. Widengren, *Mani und der Manichäismus*, 1961, 30–76, and of A. Böhlig, *Die Gnosis III. Der Manichäismus*, 1980, 21–44. This last edition contains a large number of translations from the Manichaean sources.

11. Some gnostic and related texts

1. Hippolytus, *Refutation* V, 7, 20; Origen, *Homilies on Luke* 1, 2; Eusebius, *Church History* III, 25, 6; see also n.12. However, there is also another work in the name of Thomas which deals with the miraculous events of Jesus' childhood years. This probably dates from the end of the second century; see W. Schneemelcher and R. McL. Wilson (eds), *New Testament Apocrypha* I, 1991, 439–52.
2. Oxyrhynchus Papyrus 654; other sayings in Oxyrhynchus Papyrus 1 and 655.

3. I refer to this division which was made by the first editors of this text: A. Guillaumont et al., *The Gospel according to Thomas. Coptic Text Established and Translated*, Leiden 1959.

4. See E. T. Fallon and R. Cameron, 'The Gospel of Thomas. A Forschungsbericht and Analysis', 1988, 4230–6.

5. For the Father see e.g. Gospel of Thomas (NHC II, 2) 3, 27, 40, 44, 50, 57, 61, 64, 69, 76, 79, 96–99, for God: 100, where Jesus says: 'Give Caesar what is Caesar's, give God what is God's, and give me what is mine'; cf. Matt. 22.21 and parallels.

6. Gospel of Thomas 49, 50; cf.19.

7. Gospel of Thomas 22; cf. 11, 106 and T. Baarda, *Early Transmission of Words of Jesus*, 1983, 261–88.

8. Gospel of Thomas 13.

9. Gospel of Thomas 3, 5, 17, 39, 51, 62, 69, 78, 91.

10. Gospel of Thomas 67.

11. See for example T. Baarda, *Essays on the Diatessaron*, 1994, 147–71, on Gospel of Thomas 27, where he explains 'sabbath' as the Creator/demiurge.

12. Thus Cyril of Jerusalem (fourth century), *Catechetical Lectures* 4, 36; 6, 31.

13. Thus H. Koester, *Ancient Christian Gospels. Their History and Development*, 1990, 84–6.

14. Fallon and Cameron, 'Gospel of Thomas' (n.4), 4213–30; cf. also C. M. Tuckett, 'The Gospel of Thomas: Evidence for Jesus?', 1998.

15. There is an English translation (by W. W. Isenberg) in J. M. Robinson (ed.), *The Nag Hammadi Library in English,* ⁴1996, 141–60. I refer to the pages of the codex.

16. Gospel of Philip (NHC II, 3) 56, 58, 59, 63, 64, 67.

17. See G. Sfameni Gasparro, 'Il "Vangelo secondo Filippo": rassegna degli studi e proposte di interpretazione', 1988, 4110, 4114, 4146.

18. Gospel of Philip 60; for Sophia cf. also 59; 63. The names Echamoth and Echmoth are derived from the Hebrew *ḥokhmah*, 'wisdom'; cf. p. 71.

19. Gospel of Philip 63, 71–72, 73.

20. Gospel of Philip 53, 54, 55.

21. Gospel of Philip 54, 55, 56, 59, 61, 67, 68, 71, 74, 75.

22. Gospel of Philip 55, 58, 59, 60, 64, 67, 69, 75, 77.

23. Gospel of Philip 52, 62, 74, 75.

24. Gospel of Philip 77, 82–83.

25. Gospel of Philip 51, 52, 55, 62.
26. Gospel of Philip 65, 67, 69–70, 71, 72, 74, 75–76, 82, 84–85.
27. Gospel of Philip 56–57, 66, 67, 69, 73, 74.
28. Gospel of Philip 54, 67, 84.
29. In Nag Hammadi Codex I, 3, 16–43; in fragmentary form in NHC XII, 2. There is an English translation (by H. W. Attridge and G. W. MacRae) in J. M. Robinson (ed.), *The Nag Hammadi Library in English*, ⁴1996, 40–51.
30. Irenaeus, *Against the Heresies* III, 11, 9.
31. J. Helderman, 'Das Evangelium Veritatis in der neueren Forschung', 1986, 4101, argues for this view. C. Markschies, *Valentinus Gnosticus?*, 1992, 339–56, does not think this assumption sufficiently well-founded. I still do not accept the presupposition by R. Mortley, '"The Name of the Father is the Son" (Gospel of Truth 38)', 1992, that the version in NHC 1, 3 comes from the fourth century and is directed against the Arians, though it is supported by M. Tardieu.
32. Nag Hammadi Codex I, 4, 43–50. There is an English translation (by M. Peel), in J. M. Robinson (ed.), *The Nag Hammadi Library in English*, ⁴1996, 54–7.
33. Cf. Rom. 6.4; Eph. 2.6; Col. 2.12; II Tim. 2.11–12.
34. I Cor. 15.44; see R. Roukema, *De uitleg van Paulus' eerste brief aan de Corinthiërs in de tweede en derde eeuw*, 1996, 241–59.
35. See J. É. Ménard, *Le traité sur la résurrection (NH I, 4)*, 1983, 7–10. However, M. J. Edwards, 'The *Epistle to Rheginus*: Valentinianism in the Fourth Century', thinks that a late dating, even to the fourth century, is possible.
36. There is an English translation in J. K. Elliott, *The Apocryphal New Testament. A Collection of Apocryphal Christian Literature in an English Translation*, Oxford 1993, 447–511.
37. Acts of Thomas 108–113. The song also occurs in one of the Greek manuscripts.
38. See P. H. Poirier, *L'hymne de la perle des Actes de Thomas*, 1981, 317.
39. For this see Poirier, *L'hymne de la perle* (n.38).
40. For this eagle see the Syrian Revelation of Baruch 77, 17–26; 87; IV Baruch 6.15–7.36; the Apocryphon of John 63 (p. 45).
41. See Poirier, *L'hymne de la perle* (n.38), 147, 278–9, 310–7.
42. See the conclusion by Poirier, *L'hymne de la perle* (n.38), 319–20, and K. Beyer, 'Das syrische Perlenlied. Ein Erlösungs-mythos als Märchengedicht', 1990, 241.

12. The gnosis of some church fathers

1. See p. 101 n.34 with references to the Didache, the Letter of (pseudo-) Barnabas, I Clement and Ignatius' Letter to the Ephesians; cf. also p. 59.
2. *Against the Heresies* II, 26, 1.
3. *Against the Heresies* II, 27, 1; 28, 2–9; cf. R. Roukema, *De uitleg van Paulus' eerste brief aan de Corinthiërs in de tweede en derde eeuw*, 1996, 197–8.
4. *Stromateis* II, 10, 2; cf. p. 130.
5. E.g. *Stromateis* V, 1; V, 5, 2; V, 26; VII, 55, 1–3; 95, 9; for Clement see W.Völker, *Der wahre Gnostiker nach Clemens Alexandrinus*, 1952; S. R. C. Lilla, *Clement of Alexandria. A Study in Christian Platonism and Gnosticism*, 1971.
6. E.g. *Stromateis* V, 32–40; VI, 126; 129, 4.
7. *Stromateis* VI, 61, 1–3; VII, 55, 6; *Hypotyposes* VII (in Eusebius, *Church History* II, 1, 4).
8. *Stromateis* VI, 78–80.
9. *Stromateis* II, 47, 4; IV, 40, 1; VII, 10, 1–3.
10. *Stromateis* IV, 116, 2–117, 2.
11. Clement uses this expression once, in *Stromateis* VII, 106, 3.
12. *Stromateis* II, 52, 5–6; III, 30, 1; 109, 2; VII, 106; *Tutor* I, 31, 2; 52, 2. A. Méhat, '"Vraie" et "fausse" gnose d'après Clément d'Alexandrie', 1980, rightly criticizes Lilla's conclusion (see n.5) that to an important extent Clement was dependent on the heretical gnostics.
13. *Stromateis* IV, 148, 2.
14. *Stromateis* III, 94, 2–3; IV, 165, 3–4; 167, 4: *Selections from the Prophetic Sayings*, 17; see J.Hering, *Étude sur la doctrine de la chute et de la préexistence des âmes chez Clément d'Alexandrie*, 1923, 28–34.
15. *Stromateis* II, 31, 3; 51. 3; V, 1, 3.
16. *Tutor* I, 31, 2; III, 78, 1–2.
17. See for example Origen's *Homilies on Exodus* 12.4; more texts in R. Roukema, 'La prédication du Christ crucifié (I Corinthiens 2, 2) selon Origène', 1995. See also G. af Hallström, *Fides simpliciorum according to Origen of Alexandria*, 1984.
18. In his *Commentary on John* XIX, 48 he explains the poor widow's two mites (Luke 21.2) in passing as the 'gnostic' and the 'practical', i.e. knowledge and practice. This distinction is derived from Plato, cf. p. 188 n.1.

19. Cf. *Against Celsus* V, 61.
20. Cf. J. W. Trigg, 'Origen Man of the Church', 1992.
21. *On the Principles* I, praefatio 4–10 . . . There is an introduction to this book of Origen's in L. Lies, *Origenes 'Peri Archon'. Eine undogmatische Dogmatik*, 1992.
22. *On the Principles* I, 5; I, 7–8; II, 6; II, 8.
23. *Fragments on the Psalms* CXLII (ed. Cadiou, 131); *Commentary on Ephesians* IX (ed. Gregg, *JThS* 3, 1902, 399).
24. *Homilies on Luke* 23.5–6; *Homilies on Psalm* 36, 5, 7.
25. *On the Principles* I, 6; II, 10, 1–3.
26. Cf. R. Roukema, 'Reïncarnatie in de oude kerk', 1992–1993, and '"Die Liebe kommt nie zu Fall" (I Korinther 13, 8a) als Argument des Origenes gegen einen neuen Abfall der Seelen von Gott', 1999.
27. *On the Principles* IV, 2–3.
28. Cf. the study by H. Strutwolf, *Gnosis als System. Zur Rezeption der valentianischen Gnosis bei Origenes*, 1993.
29. *On the Principles* II, 1, 4; see Lies, *Origenes 'Peri Archon'* (n.21), 84–5.
30. See R. Roukema, 'Het zelfbewustzijn van een bespotte minderheid', 1994, 47–50.
31. Translated from the Greek into French by A. and C. Guillaumont, *Évagre le Pontique. Traité Pratique ou le moine* II, 1971.
32. The Syriac versions have been edited and translated into French by A. Guillaumont, *Les six centuries des 'Kephalaia Gnostica' d'Évagre le Pontique,* 1958.
33. *Kephalaia Gnostica* I, 70; II, 47; III, 6; III, 15; III, 41; V, 62–63.
34. *Kephalaia Gnostica* I, 63; III, 38; III, 51; VI, 20; VI, 75.
35. *Kephalaia Gnostica* I, 26; I, 58; II, 17; II, 62; II, 69; II, 77; III, 25; III, 66; V, 19; VI, 57–58.
36. *Kephalaia Gnostica* II, 85; III, 9; III, 20; IV, 38; VI, 45.
37. *Gnosticus* 7 (in A. and C.Guillaumont, *Évagre le Pontique. Le Gnostique,* 1989).
38. See J. G. Bunge, 'Origenismus – Gnostizismus. Zum geistesgeschichtlichen Standort des Evagrios Pontikos', 1986.
39. See E. A. Clark, *The Origenist Controversy. The Cultural Construction of an Early Christian Debate,* 1992.
40. A. Guillaumont, *Les 'Kephalaia Gnostica' d'Évagre le Pontique et l'historie de l'origénisme chez les Grecs et chez les Syriens,* 1962.

41. The text is in E.Schwartz, *Acta Conciliorum Oecumenicorum* III, 1940, 189–214.

13. Gnosis assessed

1. See e.g. B. Aland, 'Gnosis und Kirchenväter', 1978; G. W. MacRae, *Studies in the New Testament and Gnosticism*, 1987, 251–62.
2. *Against the Heresies* III, 11, 1 (cf. p. 127); also e.g. II, 10, 2; II, 30, 9–31, 1.
3. See e.g. Irenaeus, *Against the Heresies* IV; Tertullian, *Prescription of Heretics* 13; *Against the Valentinians* 17–21; Hippolytus, *Refutation* X, 32–33; Clement, *Stromateis* II, 32, 1–2; II, 36–40; *Tutor* I, 62–74; Origen, *On the Principles* II, 4–5; III, 1, 16.
4. See J. N. D. Kelly, *Early Christian Creeds*, ³1972, 163–6.
5. See I Corinthians 15. 44; R. Roukema, *De uitleg van Paulus' eerste brief aan de Corinthiërs in de tweede en derde eeuw*, 1996, 226–60.
6. See p. 191 n.25.
7. II Peter 3, 13 with references to Isa. 65.17; 66.22.
8. The same is true of the writing Pistis Sophia, cf. p. 192 n.6.
9. There is a survey of the different views on this in the Nag Hammadi writings in M. Franzmann, *Jesus in the Nag Hammadi Writings*, 1996, 135–59.
10. *Against the Heresies* III, 11, 2–3; III, 16–23; V, 7, 1–8, 1.
11. His works *The Flesh of Christ* and the *Resurrection of the Dead* are devoted to this.
12. Hippolytus, *The Resurrection*, frags VII-VIII (ed. Achelis, GCS 1, 2, 253).
13. *On the Principles* I, praefatio 4; II, 6, 1–2; IV, 4, 3; *Commentary on John* VI, 273–275; 288–290; *Against Celsus* II, 58–61.
14. *Against Celsus* II, 62; III, 41–42.
15. *Stromateis* VI, 71, 2; the view of Valentinus is akin to this, see p. 129. Cf. also Clement, *Exhortation to the Greeks* 110, 2; 111, 2; *Stromateis* IV, 66, 4.
16. *Who is the Rich Man that is Saved?*, 33; 37; *Tutor* III, 98, 2; *Stromateis* IV, 43, 2.
17. John 18.20.
18. I Cor. 1.18–25.
19. Gospel of Thomas, superscription.

20. I Cor. 15.3–4.
21. See pp. 131, 133; also Irenaeus, *Against the Heresies* I, 5, 1; 8, 3; Tertullian, *Against the Valentinians* 19; Hippolytus, *Refutation* V, 8, 44; X, 9, 3; Clement, *Stromateis* IV, 89, 1–4; 93, 1; *Tutor* I, 31, 2; Origen, *On the Principles* I, 8, 2; III, 1, 8; 1, 23; 4, 5.
22. Cf. Gospel of Philip 77.
23. Tertullian, *Against Praxeas* 3, 1–2.
24. *Against the Heresies* IV, 33, 1; 33, 15; V, 6, 1; 8, 2–3; 9, 2.
25. *Against the Heresies* I, 10, 1–2; II, 19, 7; 26, 1; III, 3, 1; cf. also Irenaeus, *Apostolic Preaching* 4–6.
26. Porphyry, *Life of Plotinus* 16; Plotinus, *Enneads* II, 9, 6.
27. See Kelly, *Early Christian Creeds* (n.4), 385.
28. W. A. Bienert, *Dogmengeschichte*, 1997, 69; cf. 52, and Cyril of Jerusalem, *Catechetical Lectures* 18, 23.
29. Acts 11.26; I Cor. 1.26–28.

Index of texts

1 Bible

1.1 Old Testament

Genesis

1.1–2.3	65
1.2	42
1.26	33, 35, 43, 72, 83, 109, 181
1.27	82
1.28	134
1.31	108
2.4–17	66
2.4–5	84
2.4	185
2.7	84, 186
2.9	44
2.18–3.24	66
2.18	43
2.20	43
2.21–22	44
2.23–24	45
2.24	180
3	51
3.16–24	45
3.19	186
3.20	44, 45
4.1–16	66
4.1–2	45
4.21	46
4.25	41
5.1	185
5.24	186
6.1–4	47, 48, 187
6.2	186
6.5 etc.	47
12.1	180

Exodus

3.14	86, 189
13.21–22	182
14.19	182
14.24	182
20.5	182, 192
34.14	192

Numbers

14.14	182

Deuteronomy

4.24	192
4.34–35	186
5.9	182, 192
6.4	186, 188
6.13	189
6.15	192
32.8	186

I Kings

22.19	182

II Kings

2.1–11	186

Job

1.6	186
2.1	186
3.8	184
10.16	182
16.20–21	186
19.26	186
28.12–28	187
38.7	186
42.17	186

Psalms

1.5–6	186
8	69
45	27
45.7	182
45.11–12	180
47.9	182
90.3	186
103.1–5	180
104	68
104.25	184
104.29	186
110.1	135
124.8	160
146.4	186

Proverbs

2.6	74
8.22–31	187
8.22	86, 189
16.8	74

Ecclesiastes

3.20	186
3.21	186
9.10	186
12.7	186

Isaiah

14.13	71
24.1–6	186
26.19	186
27.1	184
38.13	182
45.5–6	182, 192

45.5	186	**Mark**		**Romans**	
46.9	182,	4.11	166	3.28	179
	186, 192	4.34	166	6.3	180
51.3	186			6.4	198
65.17	201	**Luke**		9–11	162
66.1	182	1.35	133	10.9	191
66.22	201	10.18	187	11.20–25	162
		11.52	190		
Jeremiah		15.3–7	20	**I Corinthians**	
3.1–4	180	21.2	199	1.18–25	201
4.23–28	186			1.26–28	202
		John		2.2	199
Ezekiel		1.1–5	194	2.9	134
1.26	182, 187	1.1–4	191	2.10	184
28.13	186	1.3	132, 182	5.9–10	180
31.9	186	1.14–18	191	6.18	180
31.16–18	186	1.14	19, 163	7.9	128
37.1–14	186	3.3	185	8.1	191
		3.15–17	179	12.3	191
Daniel		5.24	179	15.3–4	190,
7.9	187	6.40	179		191, 202
7.13–14	187	6.44	180	15.44	198, 201
10.13	187	6.63	180		
10.20–21	187	8.14	181	**Galatians**	
12.2	186	8.44	181	2.16	179
12.4	187	10.28	179	3.27	180
		13.3	181	4.21–5.1	179
Hosea		14.1–3	191	5.4–5	179
2.1–6	180	14.5–7	191		
5.14	182, 192	14.16	196	**Ephesians**	
11.10	182, 192	14.26	196	2.6	198
13.7–8	182, 192	15.26	196	2.7	181
		16.5	181	2.8	179
Joel		16.7	196	3.19	191
2.3	186	16.28	181	4.32	181
		17.2–3	179	6.12	180
		17.3	191		
1.2 New		18.20	201	**Philippians**	
Testament		20.17	181, 191	2.5–11	191
		20.31	191		
Matthew				**Colossians**	
4.21	181	**Acts of the Apostles**		2.12	198
10.2	181	6.5	178		
12.31–32	183	8.9–24	13	**I Timothy**	
13.45–46	147	11.26	202	6.20	101
19.11–12	128	14.11–12	179		
19.28	185	15.20	180	**II Timothy**	
20.20–24	181	21.8	178	2.11–12	198
22.21	197				
28.18	182			**Titus**	
				3.4–5	179

James
4.12   191

I Peter
1.12   184

II Peter
1.5–6   191
2.4   187
3.13   201
3.18   191

Jude
6   187

Revelation
12.7–12   187

2 Jewish writings

2.1 Deutero-canonical books

Tobit
3.8   187
12.15   181

II Maccabees
7   186

Wisdom of Solomon
1.4–7   187
1.13–14   186
2.13   74
2.23–24   70, 186
7.23   187
7.25–26   187
9.4   187
9.17   187
10.1–2   187
10.10   74
14.22   74
18.14–15   187

Sirach
1.1–10   187
4.11–19   187
7.15   186
24.1–22   187

Baruch
3.9–38   187

2.2 Pseud-epigrapha

Life of Adam and Eve
12–16   187

I (or Ethiopian) Enoch
6–9   187
20.7   181
46.1–5   187
48.2   187
51   186
62.5–14   187
81.5   181

Testament of Judah
25   186

Testament of Benjamin
10.6–11   186

Testament of Job
4.9–10   186
39.8–40.3   186
52.1–12   186

Psalms of Solomon
2.31   186
3.12   186

2.3 Writings of Qumran

Community Rule (1QS)
4.4   188
4.6   188

2.4 Philo of Alexandria

On the Creation
            82–4
21   189
171   188

Allegorical Interpretation
I,96   189
III,73   189
III,126   189
III,207   189

On the Cherubim
27–28   189
49–50   189
109   185
113   185
115   185

On the Sacrifices of Abel and Cain
59   189
131   191

The Worse attacks the Better
54   189
115–116   189

On the Posterity of Cain
124   189

On the Giants
12–15   189

On the Unchange-ableness of God
143   189

On Noah's Work as a planter
14   189
18–20   188
86   189

On Drunkenness
30–31   189
31   187

On the Confusion of Tongues
77–78   189
168–182   188
172   188

Who is the Heir
166   189
239–240   189
282–283   189
308–309   189

On Flight and Finding
66   191
68–72   188
82   189
94–98   189
99   191
109   189

On the Change of Names
11–14   189
28–29   189
30–32   188
100–101   189

On Dreams
I,138–139   189
I,227–230   189
II,294   189

On Abraham
121–124   189
268   189

On Moses
I,21   189
I,75–76   189
II,48   191
II,99–100   189

On the Special Laws
I,45–49   188
I,327–329   188

On the Virtues
178–179   189

On Rewards and Punishments
9   189

On the Eternity of the World
13   188

Questions on Genesis
II,62   189

Questions on Exodus
I,23   188
II,68   189

2.5 Rabbinical writings

Eighteen Benedictions
             74

Pirke Aboth
3.1   184

Aboth de Rabbi Nathan
19   185

Derek Eretz Zuta
3.9   185

Derek Eretz Rabbah
3.1   185

Babylonian Talmud Hagigah
14bc   187
15a   187

Jerusalem Talmud Sotah
2.2   185

3 Christian (including gnostic) writings

Athenagoras
Supplication
3   192

Augustine
Confessions
V,14,24   193

(pseudo-)Barnabas
1.5   191
2.3   191
14.1–6   191
15.5–16.2   191

Bruce Codex
52   183

Clement of Alexandria
Selections from the Prophetic Sayings
17   199
26,1   192

Exhortation to the Greeks
110,2   201
111,2   201

Who is the Rich Man that is Saved
33   201
37   201

Tutor
I,31,2   199, 202
I,52,2   199
I,62–74   201
I,68,2–3   192
III,78,1–2   199
III,98,2   201

Stromateis
II,10   194
II,10,2   195, 199
II,27,2   194
II,31,3   199
II,32,1–2   201
II,36–40   201
II,36,1   194
II,36,2–4   195
II,47,4   199
II,51,3   199
II,52,5–6   199
III,1–3   194
III,30,1   199
III,59,3   195
III,40   192
III,94,2–3   199
III,109,2   199
IV,40,1   199
IV,43,2   201
IV,66,4   201
IV,71,1   195
IV,81–83   194
IV,86,1   194
IV,89,1–4   202

IV,93,1 202
IV,116,2–
  117,2 199
IV,148,2 199
IV,153,4 194
IV,165,
  3–4 199
IV,165,3 194
IV,167,4 199
V,1 199
V,1,3 199
V,3,2 194
V,5,2 199
V,26 199
V,32–40 199
V,74,3 194
VI,61,1–3 199
VI,71,2 201
VI,78–80 199
VI,126 199
VI,129,4 199
VII,10,1–3 199
VII,55,1–3 199
VII,55,6 199
VII,95,9 199
VII,106 199
VII,106,
  3–4 194
VII,106,3 199
VII,106,
  4–107,1 196
VII,106,4 194

Hypotyposes
VII 199

Excerpts from Theodotus
1,1 195
28 194
35,1–2 195
58–60 195
61–62 195
69,1–78,1 185
78,2 185

Clement of Rome
I Clement
1.2 191

36.2 191
38.3 184
38.4 184
40.1 184, 191
41.4 191
48.5 191

Cyril of Jerusalem
Catechetical Lectures
4,36 197
6,31 197
18,23 202

Didache
9.3 191
10.2 191
11.2 191

Epiphanius
Panarion
21,1–4 178
21,2,4 179
21,3,3 179
21,3,4 179
22 179
23 181
23,1,7 181
26,3,3 192
26,4–5 192
26,9,6–9 192
26,17,4 192
31,2,1–3 194
31,7,1–2 194
31,32 195
33,3–8 195
36,3,2 183
41,1,1–9 196
42,1,3–4 196
42,1,4 196

Eusebius
Church History
II,1,4 199
III,25,6 196
IV,11,1 194–195
IV,14,6 194
IV,14,7 196

Preparation for the Gospel
IX,29 187

Evagrius of Pontus
Gnosticus
7 200

Kephalaia Gnostica
156, 200

Hippolytus
Refutation of all Heresies
V,2 193
V,7,20 196
V,8,44 202
V,23–27 195
V,27,5 196
VI,3 193
VI,19,
  1–20,2 178
VI,19,5 179
VI,21–29 193
VI,35,5–6 195
VII,14–20 193
VII,20–27 194
VII,20,1 194
VII,28 181
VII,28,5 181
VII,33 194
X,9,3 202
X,14 194
X,21 194
X,32–33 201

The Resurrection of the Dead
fr. VII–VIII 201

Ignatius of Antioch
Ephesians
superscription
  191
7.2 191
17.2 191

Magnesians
8.1 191
9.1 191

10.3　　　191

Trallians
9　　　191

Irenaeus
Apostolic Preaching
4–6　　　202

Against the Heresies
I, praefatio
　1　　　191
I, praefatio
　2　　　195
I,1–9　　　195
I,5,1　　　202
I,5,2　　　185
I,6,3　　　192
I,8,3　　　202
I,10,1–2　　　202
I,11,1　　　194, 195
I,13,3–7　　　192
I,21,5　　　183
I,22,2　　　178
I,23　　　178
I,23,2　　　178
I,23,4　　　192
I,23,5　　　179
I,24,1　　　180
I,24,1–2　　　181
I,24,3–7　　　194
I,25,3–5　　　192
I,26,1　　　194
I,27,1　　　196
I,27,3　　　196
I,29　　　181
I,29,1　　　180
I,29,3　　　182
I,29,4　　　182
I,30　　　183
I,30,5　　　183
I,30,6　　　183
II, praefatio
　1　　　180
II,10,2　　　201
II,14,1–6　　　193
II,19,7　　　202
II,26,1　　　199, 202
II,27,1　　　199

II,28,2–9　　　199
II,30,9–
　31,1　　　201
II,31,1　　　196
II,32,1–2　　　192
III,3,1　　　202
III,3,4　　　194, 196
III,4,3　　　194, 196
III,11,1　　　194, 201
III,11,2–3　　　201
III,11,2　　　180
III,11,9　　　198
III,16–23　　　201
III,16,1　　　193
IV,6,4　　　196
IV,33,1　　　202
IV,33,2　　　196
IV,33,15　　　202
V,6,1　　　202
V,7,1–8,1　　　201
V,8,2–3　　　202
V,9,2　　　202

Justin Martyr
Dialogue with the Jew Trypho
120,6　　　178

First Apology
26,2–5　　　196
26,2–3　　　178
26,4　　　179
26,7　　　192
26,8　　　178
27,5　　　192
64,5　　　179

Second Apology
12,1–2　　　192

Minucius Felix
Octavius
9　　　192

Nag Hammadi Codices
Gospel of Truth
(NHC I,3; XII,2)
　　　143–4, 198

Treatise on the Resurrection (NHC I,4)
　　　145, 198

Secret Book
(Apocryphon) of John
(NHC II,1; III,1; IV,1; BG 8502)
　　　38–48
NHC II,1, 21,11
　　　180

Gospel of Thomas
(NHC II,2)
　　　140–2, 197

Superscription
　　　201
76　　　147

Gospel of Philip
(NHC II,3)
　　　142–3, 197–8
53–54　　　192
66　　　192
77　　　202

Origin of the World
(NHC II,5)
103　　　183

Exegesis on the Soul
(NHC II,6)
　　　26–8, 181

Revelation of Paul
(NHC V,2)
20–23　　　184

First Revelation of James (NHC V,3)
33–34　　　183

Apocalypse of Adam
(NHC V,5)
　　　193

The Thunder: Perfect
Mind (NHC VI,2)
14   192
19   192

Origen
On the Principles
I, praefatio
  4–10   200
I, praefatio
  4   201
I,5   200
I,6   200
I,7–8   200
I,8,2   202
II,1,4   200
II,4–5   201
II,5,1–3   192–3
II,6   200
II,6,1–2   201
II,8   200
II,10,1–3   200
III,1,8   202
III,1,16   201
III,1,23   202
III,4,5   202
IV,2–3   200
IV,2,1   193
IV,4,3   201

Homilies on Exodus
6,9   196
8,5   193
12,4   199

*Homilies on the
Psalms*
36,5,7   200

*Fragments on the
Psalms* (ed. Cadiou)
CXLII   200

*Commentary on
Matthew*
XVII,19   193

Homilies on Luke
1,2   196
23,5–6   200

Commentary on John
II,73–75   195
II,100–104 195
VI,273–
  275   201
VI,288–
  290   201
XIX,48   199

*Commentary on
Ephesians* (ed. Gregg)
IX   200

Against Celsus
II,58–61   201
II,62   201
III,12   193
III,41–42   201
V,59   178
V,61   200
V,62   178
VI,22–32   183
VI,25   184
VI,31   183, 184
VI,32   183

Tertullian
Apologeticum
7–8   192

*The Prescription of
Heretics*
7,1–4   185
7,2–11   193
7,5   185
7,6   185
13   201
30,1–3   196

Against Marcion
I,11,9   196
I,19,4   196
II,5,1   196
II,9,1   196
III,8,2–7   196
V,6,11   196

*Against the
Valentinians*
I,4   193

4,1   194, 195
4,2   195
4,3   195
17–21   201
19   202

On the Soul
23,1   181
34   178
34,3   178
50,2–5   179

Against Praxeas
3,1–2   202

Acts of Thomas
108–113   145–8,
            198

4 Greek and
Roman authors

Alcinous
*Handbook on the
Teaching of Plato*
            88–9,
            189

Apuleius
*Metamorphoses (The
Golden Ass)*
            96–7,
            190

Calcidius
*Commentary on the
Timaeus*
295–299   189

Cicero
Republic
VI,16–17   183

Corpus Hermeticum
I   193

Homer
Odyssey
IV,261–264 180

Numenius
Fragments 89–91,
            189–190

Ovid
Metamorphoses
VIII,626–724 179

Plato
Euthyphro
2a–3b   188

Apology
23cd   188
24bc   188

Phaedo
64c–69c   188
72e–77a   188
79ab   188
80a   188
97c–98b   188
102a   188
103e   188
114bc   179, 183

Cratylus
400bc   179
400c   183
439c–440b   188

Theaetetus
149a–151b   188
155d   188
176b   188

Statesman
258e–261b   188

Parmenides
128e–135c   188
137c–166c   188

Philebus
28c–31a   188

Symposium
210e–212b   188
211a–212b   188

Phaedrus
243ab   179
246a–247e   188
247cd   188
249c–250c   188

Meno
73e–76e   188
81c–85d   188

Republic
379a–380c   188
476c–478c   188
484c   188
502d–509c   188
508e   188
517b–521b   188
517b–520c   188
527b   188
586c   179
596b–597e   188
596cd   188
613a–621d   179
613a   188
616c   189
619e–621d   188

Timaeus   77–9
30ab   188
39e   188
41d–52b   179
46b–47b   188

Laws
896e   189

897d   189

Letters
VII,341b–344d
     188

Plotinus
Enneads
II,9,6   192,
     193, 202
II,9,15–17   192
II,9,17   193
VI,9,9   180

Plutarch
Isis and Osiris
     108–9,
     190

Porphyry
Life of Plotinus
16   202

Proclus
*Commentary on
Plato's Republic*
XVI,128–
     132   189

Seneca
Letters to Lucilius
65,19–20   184
82,5–6   184

Naturales Quaestiones
III, praefatio
     10–18   184

Index of names and subjects

Abel 45, 48, 66–7, 137
Abraham 27, 30, 98, 159
Adam 40–1, 43–5, 47–9, 51, 66,
    68, 71, 108–11, 129, 134–5,
    139, 163, 180, 182, 183
Akabya ben Mahalalel 59–60
Alcinous 88–92, 109–10
Apuleius 95–7, 119
Aristotle 57, 62, 82, 193
astrology 42, 61–2
Athene 17, 20, 108
Augustine 139, 193

baptism 23–4, 27, 61–2, 100, 185
Barbelo 39–40, 46, 49
Basilides 7, 9, 33, 127–9, 136
Berlin Codex 6, 37–8

Cain 45, 48, 66–8, 137
Carpocrates 9, 24
Celsus 9, 118, 178
Cerdo 24, 136
Cerinthus 7, 24, 126–7, 164
Clement of Alexandria 9, 61, 124,
    127–30, 133, 151–3, 157,
    159–60, 164, 168–9
Clement of Rome 59
Cronus 78, 182

devil (see also Satan) 70, 73, 131,
    154, 181
docetism 20, 33, 36, 50, 113–14,
    136, 163–4, 167, 179

Ebionites 24
Elisha ben Abuyah 73

Elohim (Eloim) 45, 65, 134–5
Enoch 73, 137, 186
Epicurus 62
Epiphanius 10, 13, 129, 131, 136
Evagrius 156–7
Eve 43–5, 48, 51, 66, 68, 108,
    111, 134–5, 139, 183

fate (fortune) 18, 22, 47, 58, 61–2,
    78, 89, 92, 96–7, 109, 115
First Thought 15–18, 20–1, 23, 28,
    34, 39, 105–6, 108–9, 115, 119,
    121

Helen (in Troy) 15, 21, 28
Helen (of Tyre) 15–22, 26, 111
Heracleon 9, 132–3
Hermes 119–20, 179
Hippolytus 8, 10, 13, 33, 127–30,
    133–6, 159, 163, 168
Homer 28, 31

Irenaeus 7–8, 10, 13–25, 32–7, 51,
    126–32, 136, 143–4, 163, 168–9
Isidore 9, 128
Isis 93–7, 119, 135

James (brother of Jesus) 50
John (apostle) 14, 38–9, 44, 46–9,
    127, 164
Justin the Gnostic 134–6, 164
Justin Martyr 14, 17, 23, 178

Kronos see Cronus

Leviathan 52, 69, 184

Mani 138–9
Marcion 24, 136–7
Marcionites 137, 138
Mark the Gnostic 51
Mary (mother of Jesus) 98, 126, 131, 133
Mary Magdalene 6
Menander of Antioch 23–5, 32–4, 106, 112, 121, 127, 136
Metatron 73
Montanists 8, 169
Montanus 8
Moses 44, 47, 60, 64, 72, 89, 98–100, 109, 131, 135–6, 145, 159, 166
Mother (divine) 15, 17–18, 39, 46–9, 86, 105–6, 108, 112, 130, 138, 144, 187

Nag Hammadi Codex 4–5, 26, 37–8, 140, 142–3, 145, 157, 166
Nicolaus 24
Noah 47, 137
Numenius 89–92, 109–10

Odysseus 28
Ophites 24, 51–2, 106
Origen 8, 51, 117–18, 129–30, 132, 153–7, 159–60, 164, 168–9
Osiris 93–7, 119

Paul 20, 100, 129, 137, 139, 145, 151, 153, 160, 162, 167, 179
Peter 14, 128,
Philip (apostle) 142–3
Philip (evangelist) 14, 178
Philo 60–1, 81–8, 107–8, 110, 117–18, 121, 129
Plato 21, 35–6, 44, 57, 62, 75–92, 107, 109, 118–21, 157, 169, 199
Plotinus 31, 115, 122–3, 169, 192–3
Plutarch 94–5, 119, 121
Polycarp 136
Ptolemaeus 7, 24, 130–2, 163, 168

Pythagoras 89–90

rebirth 28, 61–2, 96, 185
reincarnation 15, 18, 21, 46, 53, 58, 76–9, 81, 87, 89, 114, 119, 127, 139, 190, 192
resurrection 23, 28, 38, 69–70, 98–9, 111, 113, 133, 143–5, 153–4, 156, 160–1, 163–4, 166–7

Satan 34–6, 70–1, 108, 114
Satornilus 24, 32–6, 106, 110, 112–14, 117, 121
Seneca 57–8, 62
Seth 41, 46–9, 108
Simon the Magician 7, 13–26, 33, 105, 108, 111–13, 118–19, 136
Simonians 16–24, 30, 32, 34, 107, 111–12, 114, 119, 121
Socrates 75–7, 79–80
Sophia 40–3, 106, 108–9, 115, 121, 131, 133, 166, 182
Stesichorus 15, 21
Stoics 57, 62, 82, 193

Tertullian 8, 13, 62–3, 129–30, 159, 163, 168–9
Theodotus 9, 61–2, 111, 133–4, 163, 168
Thomas 101, 140–2, 145–7, 164–5, 196

Valentinians 129–30, 143–5, 151, 168
Valentinus 7, 9, 24, 61, 63, 129–30, 136, 143–4

Yahwe (Yao; Yaue) 19, 42, 45, 51–2, 65, 70, 109
Yaldabaoth 41–7, 49, 51–2, 106, 109–10, 114, 166

Zeus 17, 20, 78, 108, 179